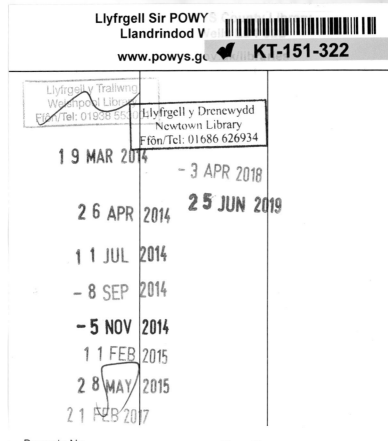
England

www.babanibooks.com

Please Note

Although every care has been taken with the production of this book to ensure that all information is correct at the time of writing and that any projects, designs, modifications and/or programs, etc., contained herewith, operate in a correct and safe manner and also that any components specified are normally available in Great Britain, the Publishers and Author(s) do not accept responsibility in any way for the failure (including fault in design) of any project, design, modification or program to work correctly or to cause damage to any equipment that it may be connected to or used in conjunction with, or in respect of any other damage or injury that may be so caused, nor do the Publishers accept responsibility in any way for the failure to obtain specified components.

Notice is also given that if equipment that is still under warranty is modified in any way or used or connected with home-built equipment then that warranty may be void.

© 2014 BERNARD BABANI (publishing) LTD

First Published - January 2014

British Library Cataloguing in Publication Data:

A catalogue record for this book is available from the British Library

ISBN 978 0 85934 743 3

Cover Design by Gregor Arthur

Printed and bound in Great Britain for Bernard Babani (publishing) Ltd

About this Book

Kindle Fire HDX Explained has been written to help users get to grips, as quickly as possible, with Amazon's latest versions of their Fire tablet.

This book applies to the

* Kindle Fire HDX 7" display tablet,
* Kindle Fire HDX 8.9" display tablet.

Both HDX tablets optimise screen quality, have outstanding audio, more space to accommodate large files and faster processors (HDX almost double that of the earlier HD model) which increases the speed of downloading Web pages and video streaming. Both the HDX 7" and the HDX 8.9" specifications are such that they minimise screen glare, optimise colour sharpness and give the correct conditions for looking at photos, films and other information at a much wider angle without any distortion.

Both Kindle Fire HDX models come with stereo Bluetooth for connecting with compatible Bluetooth headphones and keyboards. Even the WiFi connection comes with dual-antenna and dual-band for better range reception.

You can use these latest two Kindle models to read books and magazines, play music and games, listen to e-books and even watch films using Amazon's LoveFilm subscription subsidiary.

Both Kindle Fire HDX models use the Amazon Whispersync technology to automatically synchronise your library, the last page read, your bookmarks, notes and highlights across all your devices. With Kindle reading Apps available for phones, tablets, PCs and Macs, you can keep in touch wherever you are and with whichever device you are using at the time.

Your Kindle Fire HDXs can be used to send and receive e-mail messages that synchronise with your Gmail, Outlook and other accounts, and fully integrate with Facebook for staying in touch with friends and family. You can also use Kindle HDX's facing camera for taking photos, videos and use Skype video chats. The HDX 8.9" model has an additional back facing camera which makes it a lot easier to take photos and videos, but this book is based on the HDX 7" model.

Key Features of Kindle Fire HDX

The Kindle Fire HDX 7-inch IPS screen has a resolution of 1,920 x 1,200 pixels. It has a Quad-core 2.2 GHz Snapdragon 800 processor with 2 GB RAM, an improved Adreno 330 graphics processor, Custom Amazon UI (User Interface), the Fire 3.0. Android Mojito OS (Operating System), a 4,550 mAh battery which boast 11 hours of battery life., a 720p front-facing camera and is available with 16/32/64 GB internal memory. Unfortunately, the second screen feature, called 'Fling', for transfering info to a TV only works with PlayStation 3 and the latest model of Samsung TV. There is no HDMI port on the HDX model.

Above all, you don't have to worry how much storage is required for all your activities because everything is stored in Amazon's Cloud and is available to you for downloading to any of your devices. The only time storage on your device might become an issue is if you downloaded, say, several thousand books, an equal number of photos, videos and music all at once to your device!

This book will guide you through the configuration and use of Kindle Fire HDX in detail. The aim is to present the Kindle HDX's capabilities in the shortest and most effective way so that you can enjoy using it!

About the Author

Noel Kantaris graduated in Electrical Engineering at Bristol University and after spending three years in the Electronics Industry in London, took up a Tutorship in Physics at the University of Queensland. Research interests in Ionospheric Physics, led to the degrees of M.E. in Electronics and Ph.D. in Physics. On return to the UK, he took up a Post-Doctoral Research Fellowship in Radio Physics at the University of Leicester, and then a lecturing position in Engineering at the Camborne School of Mines, Cornwall, (part of Exeter University), where he was also the CSM Computing Manager. Lately he also served as IT Director of FFC Ltd.

Books by the Same Author

BP747   Windows 8.1 Explained
BP743   Kindle Fire HDX Explained
BP741   Microsoft Office 2013 Explained
BP738   Google for the Older Generation
BP735   Windows 8 Explained

More Recent Books Written with Phil Oliver

BP726   Microsoft Excel 2010 Explained
BP719   Microsoft Office 2010 Explained
BP718   Windows 7 Explained
BP710   An Introduction to Windows Live Essentials
BP706   An Introduction to Windows 7
BP703   An Introduction to Windows Vista

Trademarks

Apple Mac is either a registered trademark or a trademark of **Apple Corporation**.

Google, **Google+**, **Chrome** and **Gmail** are either registered trademarks or trademarks of **Google**.

Kindle, **Kindle Fire HDX** and **LoveFilm** are either registered trademarks or trademarks of **Amazon**.

Microsoft Office is either a registered trademark or a trademark of **Microsoft Corporation**.

OfficeSuite and **OfficeSuite Pro** are either registered trademarks or trademarks of **Mobile Systems Inc**.

Wi-Fi is a trademark of the **Wi-Fi Alliance**.

All other brand and product names used in the book are recognised as trademarks, or registered trademarks, of their respective companies.

Contents

1

Overview of Kindle Fire HDX

The front view of the Kindle is shown below with annotations:

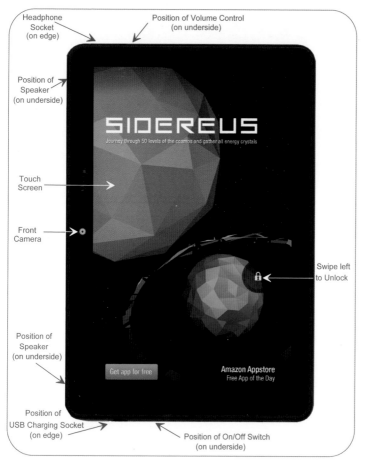

Fig. 1.1 Front View of the Kindle Fire HDX.

With the Kindle Fire HDX held in landscape orientation, so that you can read the Amazon logo, it should now look as in Fig. 1.2 with the two speakers on the top bevelled side, as shown below.

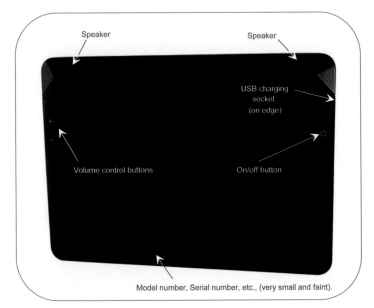

Fig. 1.2 Back View of the Kindle Fire HDX.

Starting the Kindle Fire

When you first switch on your Kindle Fire HDX it might be a good idea to plug it into a power source, using the connecting cable provided, in order to charge it up. The power source can either be a USB port on your PC or the provided mains adaptor plug shown here, in which you can plug the USB cable (also provided) to give you a much faster charging time.

After switching on your Kindle, the Setup procedure starts and first asks you to select your language, then your region, as shown in Fig. 1.3 below (only the top-half of the screen is shown).

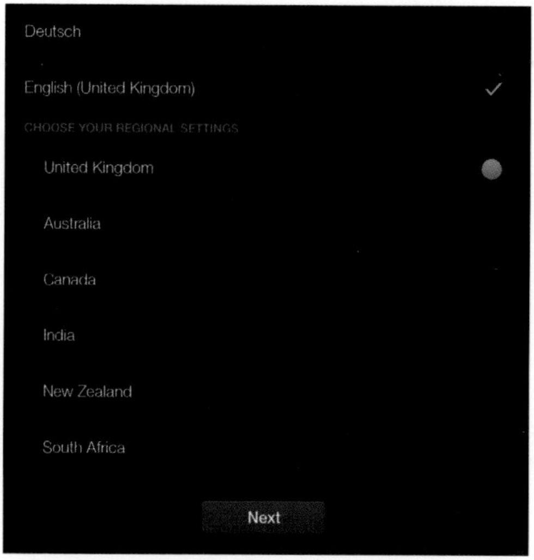

Deutsch

English (United Kingdom)   ✓

CHOOSE YOUR REGIONAL SETTINGS

United Kingdom   ⬤

Australia

Canada

India

New Zealand

South Africa

Next

Fig. 1.3 Selecting your Region.

Connecting to a Wireless Network

Tapping the **Continue** button displays the next Setup screen. The Kindle Fire HDX automatically finds all WiFi (wireless) networks in your vicinity and asks you to select the one belonging to you, as shown in Fig. 1.4 on the next page. Obviously your displayed WiFi connections will be different to those shown on the next page!

Next, select the WiFi connection that belongs to you. If there is a padlock against your selection, you'll need to type the WiFi wireless key in the displayed screen on the next page. Your WiFi key might have both lowercase and uppercase letters, as well as numbers. To type uppercase letters, tap the **Shift** key first before tapping the actual letter.

To type numbers, tap the **Numeric** key which changes the on-screen keyboard into a numeric and other symbols keyboard and at the same time replaces the **Numeric** key with the **Alphabetic** key shown here. Tapping this key returns the keyboard to its original layout as shown above. If you make any mistake, tap the **Backspace** key.

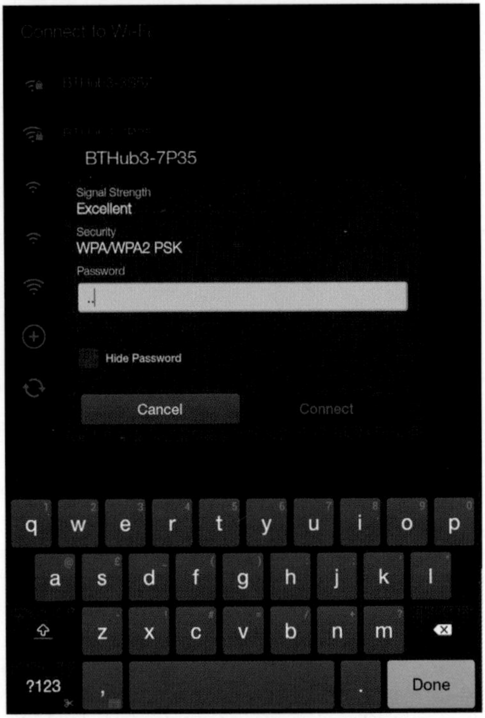

Fig. 1.4 Selecting your WiFi Connection.

Having typed in your wireless key, the **Connect** button becomes available for you to tap, which completes the connection to your WiFi.

The next Setup screen asks you to register your device, as shown in Fig. 1.5 on the next page.

Registering Your Kindle

If you already have an account with Amazon, go ahead and provide the information asked – the e-mail address used with Amazon and the password.

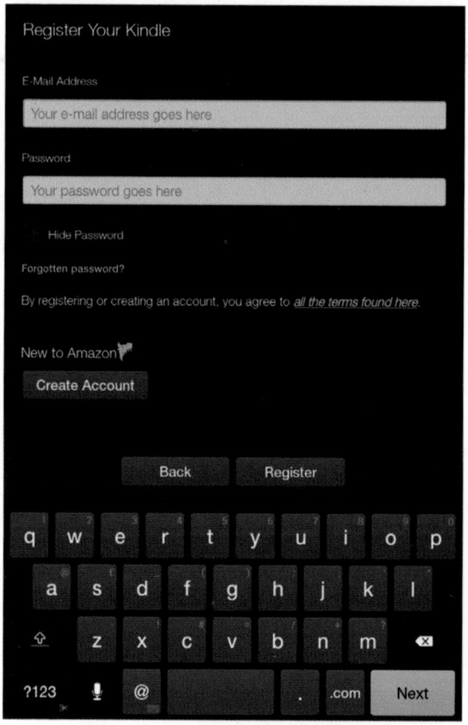

Fig. 1.5 Registering your Kindle.

If you don't have an account with Amazon, you are given the opportunity to create one by tapping the **Create Account** button. Confirmation is required.

It is important to have such an account because you need to establish a '1-click' purchase facility with Amazon (see next chapter how to do this) so as to get all the Apps you would need in the future to make your Kindle more effective, easier to use and quicker.

Connecting to Social Networks

The relevant top half of the final screen to appear in the initial Setup procedure is shown in Fig. 1.6 below.

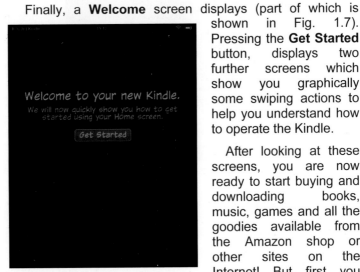

Fig. 1.6 Connecting to Social Networks.

You can join the two social networks listed straightaway, if you have your ID and Password handy.

Finally, a **Welcome** screen displays (part of which is shown in Fig. 1.7). Pressing the **Get Started** button, displays two further screens which show you graphically some swiping actions to help you understand how to operate the Kindle.

Fig. 1.7 The Welcome Screen.

After looking at these screens, you are now ready to start buying and downloading books, music, games and all the goodies available from the Amazon shop or other sites on the Internet! But first you need to familiarise yourself with the Kindle's appearance and its various settings which is part of the subject covered in the next chapter.

De-registering a Kindle

If you bought the Kindle for a friend, then you can de-register it easily if you don't want the person receiving it to have access to your stored information on the cloud. You can de-register in two ways:

The first method is by going to www.amazon.co.uk, logging into your account and scrolling down to **Manage Your Kindle**, pointed to at the bottom right-hand side in Fig. 1.8. You could use the Kindle or your PC to do this.

Fig. 1.8 De-registering a Kindle.

On the newly displayed screen, scroll down and tap/click the **Manage Your Devices** link on the left of the screen, select the Kindle in question and use the **Deregister** link. You can even change the name of your Kindle by tapping or clicking the **Edit** next to the Kindle you want to rename.

The second method requires you to do the following: First tap the **Home** 🏠 icon, then swipe from the edge of the Kindle that displays the time towards the middle of the screen to display the **Device Control Screen** (see page 23 in the next chapter), select **Settings**, then **My Account**, followed by tapping or clicking the **Deregister** button.

Protecting Your Kindle

Suggestion: To protect your Kindle from damage, I suggest you buy a leather cover for it – the type that comes with a capacitive stylus as a freebie (to avoid screen smudges) and one that  has a magnetic cover which when closed puts your Kindle to sleep.

Lifting a magnetic cover awakens your Kindle instantly and takes you back to what you were doing a lot faster than switching it off each time you take a break.

Do make sure you choose the right size cover for your particular Kindle Fire HDX model.

Such a combination (a cover and a capacitive stylus) should not cost more than around £5 from an Internet site, even though the same product is offered for more than 5 times that price by some major Internet sites!

2

Exploring Your Kindle Fire

Having completed Setup the Kindle screen changes to:

Fig. 2.1 The Welcome to Kindle Fire HDX Screen.

Searching for Books

If you tap the **Search** 🔍 icon, an on-screen keyboard is displayed as shown in Fig. 2.2 below.

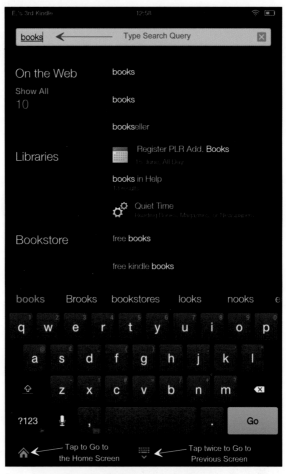

Fig. 2.2 Initiating a Search Query.

Typing a query in the **Search** box, displays returns from the **Web**, **Libraries** and **Bookstore**, as shown above. If you tap the **Home** icon, the **Home** screen is displayed as in Fig. 2.1.

Not all books from the **Bookstore** are visible because of the presence of the on-screen keyboard. Touching the screen lightly and pushing it upwards closes down the keyboard and reveals a screen similar to that in Fig. 2.3.

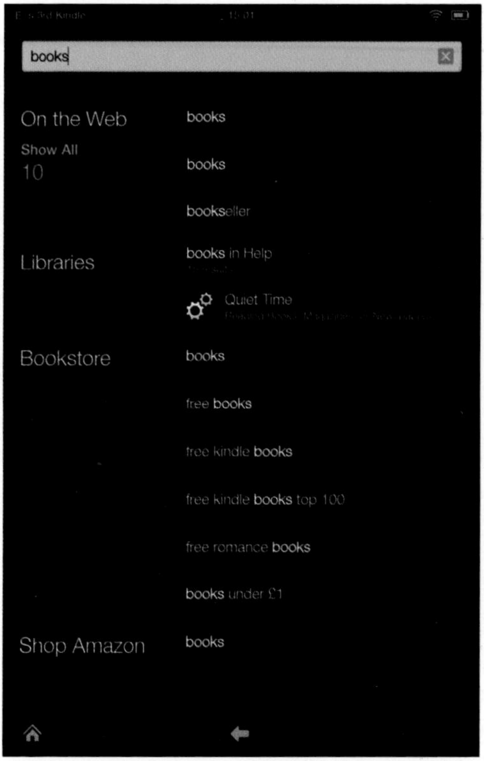

Fig. 2.3 The Full Search Results for Books in the Stores Area.

At this stage, try tapping the entry 'free kindle books'. True, there are lots of very good books in 'Kindle Books' for free and it might be a good time to have a look at some of these. You will be surprised at what is available.

If, however, you want to choose books for which you'll need to pay Amazon, then you'll need to arrange for a **1-Click** account to be set up, as discussed next.

The 1-Click Amazon Account

To set up a method of payment for your purchases with Amazon, you'll need to visit the Amazon Web site, using either your Kindle Fire (tap the **Web** library link to display Fig. 2.3, then **Search** for 'Amazon') or use your PC.

If you use your Kindle Fire to go to Amazon's Web site (or any other Web site for that matter), what is displayed on your screen is in such a small font size that you can hardly see it.

However, just like with most touch screens these days, you can use your fingers on the Kindle's screen to zoom in or out in order to make what is displayed on your screen bigger or smaller.

Zooming In or Out

To zoom in or out, place two fingers on the screen, as shown in Fig. 2.4 below and push them apart to zoom in (make what displays on the screen bigger) or pinch two fingers together to zoom out (make what displays on the screen smaller).

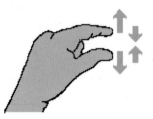

Fig. 2.4 Using Fingers to Zoom In or Out.

Next, log-in to your Amazon account, scroll down to **Settings**, then select the **1-Click Settings**, pointed to in Fig. 2.5 on the next page, but with vital information such as name, address, payment method, etc., removed for security reasons.

Your Account

Payment & GC	**Payment Methods**	**Gift Certificates**
Credit Cards & Gift Cards	Manage your Payment Methods	View Gift Card Balance
	Add a Credit Card	Apply a Gift Certificate to Your Account
	Turn On / Turn Off Amazon Currency Converter	Manage Scheduled E-Mail Gift Certificates
	Amazon Credit Cards	Manage Bulk Gift Certificate Orders
		Purchase a Gift Certificate
Settings	**Account Settings**	**Address Book**
Password, Prime & E-mail	Change Name, E-mail Address, or Password	Manage Address Book
	Forgot Your Password?	Add New Address
	1-Click Settings	**E-mail from Amazon**
	Manage Prime Membership	E-mail Preferences & Notifications
	Amazon Family Membership	AmazonLocal and Amazon Delivers E-mail Subscriptions
	Manage Your Kindle	

Fig. 2.5 The 1-Click Account Settings.

The above screen normally displays with your name, address (both blocked off), 1-Click preference, etc. Each one of which can be changed by selecting it, then tapping the **Change** button that displays on a new screen and following the on-screen instructions.

What is 1-Click? It is a fast and easy method to place an order with Amazon and pay with one tap or one click. 1-Click is automatically enabled after placing your first order. All you need to do is tap or click the 'Buy it now with 1-Click' button on the right-hand side of the 'Product Detail' page. Gifts can be sent with 1-Click by ticking the 'Add gift-wrap/message' check box under the 'Buy It Now With 1-Click' button.

Go on and create a **1-Click** account with Amazon, unless you prefer to enter your name and address and payment method for each and every transaction you make with Amazon!

Buying and Downloading

Whether you bought books, music or games and paid for them or took advantage of the free content in Amazon's Web site for Kindle books, when you choose such an item and you have gone though the process of purchasing it, it is then loaded into your 'Cloud' space allocated automatically to you by Amazon.

Items in your 'Cloud', cannot be deleted, but are there ready to be downloaded on to any of your Kindle enabled devices, such as a Windows 8 laptop, an Android tablet or an iPad. All you need to do is download into these devices a Kindle App from their supported **App** store.

To get the contents of a book, music or game from the cloud to your device, you need to be connected to a wireless network and to initiate the download. Once on your device you can read the book, listen to the music or play the game at any time without having to be connected to a WiFi network. You only need connection to the Internet to buy and download your purchased item onto your device.

As an example, I show in Fig. 2.6 on the next page some of the books in my Amazon **Cloud**. To get to this screen, simply tap the **Books library** (see Fig. 2.1 on page 9). To get to the screen displayed in Fig. 2.1, tap the **Home** icon at the bottom left of the Kindle screen, then scroll horizontally (if necessary) to the **Books library** and tap on it.

Note that at the top of the screen in Fig. 2.6, the entry **Cloud** is highlighted with an orange colour underline indicating that it is selected and what appears on the screen is what is stored (for me) on the **Cloud**. Next to the **Cloud** option the **Device** option appears, but is greyed out indicating that it is not selected.

Also note that some of the books on the **Cloud** display with a tick against their entry which indicates that they have already been downloaded to the **Device** being used at the moment. Now tapping **Device**, selects it and opens a screen showing what is (in this case) on the **Device** I'm using, shown in Fig. 2.7 on page 16.

Fig. 2.6 My Books Library on the Cloud.

Note that items on the **Cloud** are listed **By Recent** purchases (as above). You could, of course, choose to list them alphabetically **By Title** or **By Author**.

Alternatively, you could tap the **Search** 🔍 icon at the bottom of the screen to display a **Search** box and an on-screen keyboard. Such a search could be applied to the **Web**, to the **Libraries** or the **Bookstore**, if you touch the screen lightly and push it upwards to remove the keyboard from the screen, this then allows you to see the entry **Search**

everywhere, as shown here when searching for 'Tyler'.

Fig. 2.7 My Books Library on my Device in Grid View.

Tapping the **Go Back** button takes you back to the previously displayed screen.

Viewing Options

Tapping the **View** ▤ button displays an options menu, as shown here which allows you to list displayed items in **List View**, as shown in Fig. 2.8 on the next page. Also note that now the **View** menu, if you were to action it, offers you the option to return to the **Grid View**.

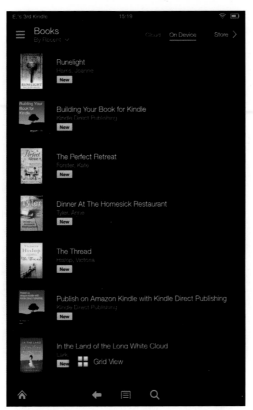

Fig. 2.8 My Books Library Listed in List View.

Getting Help

At this point I suggest you tap the **Home** icon at the bottom of the above screen, followed by the **Apps Library** option. Next, tap the displayed **Help** App shown here to open a screen in which you tap on **User Guide** to display Fig. 2.9 shown on the next page.

Do spend some time examining the various help topics that display. You could always come back to it whenever you need to know something you can't find in this book.

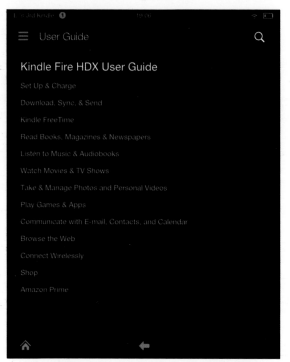

Fig. 2.9 The Help App Opening Screen.

While on the subject of help, there is a new **Help** facility that comes with the Kindle Fire HDX, called **Mayday**. However, to access this facility requires you to know a bit more about the Kindle, for example how to access the **Device Control Screen**, which will be discussed towards the end of this chapter, as will **Mayday**.

The Kindle Free Time Facility

This is a new facility from Amazon which allows you to use content you purchased to create a personalised interface for each of your children. It allows them to have their individual Kindle environment, but the parent can retain complete control of what each child can or cannot access.

For example, **Kindle FreeTime** allows the parent to block a child's access to Web browsing, browsing and purchasing from Amazon stores, block access to specified social networks and a lot more besides. It is worth exploring.

To access **Kindle FreeTime**, tap the **Home** 🏠 icon, followed by the **Apps Library** option. Next, tap the displayed **Kindle FreeTime** icon shown here to open the screen shown in Fig. 2.10 below.

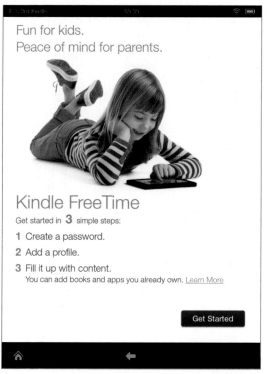

Fig. 2.10 The Kindle FreeTime Screen.

To find out exactly what this App can do, tap the **Learn More** link. To start the App and configure it, then tap the **Get Started** button to display the next **Parental Control** screen to create a password. If you have children it is worth trying it!

The Carousel

Every time you tap the **Home** ⌂ button, the Kindle returns to the starting **Home** screen with the **Carousel** displayed in the middle of the screen, the various **Library** links at the top and the **Starting** plus your purchased and installed Apps at the bottom, as shown in Fig. 2.11 below.

Fig. 2.11 The Home Screen with the Carousel.

Touching for a second a book on the **Carousel**, displays the menu shown here. You can use this menu to organise items on the **Carousel** by selecting **Add to Home**, **Remove from Device** or **Add to Collection** (a named list of books on your device). If you are touching an App on the **Carousel**, an option to **Remove from Carousel** will be displayed. Items you delete from your device always remain in the **Cloud**.

Note: The items displayed below the **Carousel** are Amazon's notifications or recommendations which change to reflect the item focused on the **Carousel.**

The Installed Apps

Tapping the **Home**  button followed by the **Apps library** link displays a screen similar to that in Fig. 2.12 below.

Fig. 2.12 The Starting and Installed Apps Screen.

The **Starting** Apps are those standard Apps that came with the Kindle Fire HDX. To see all the Apps, **Starting** plus what you purchased, loaded and installed to your device, tap the **Cloud** link to display a screen similar to that shown in Fig. 2.13 on the next page.

Fig. 2.13 All My Apps on the Cloud.

Obviously what you'll see on your screen will depend on what additional Apps you purchased and it is bound to be different from the screen above.

Do note that some Apps in Fig. 2.13, have a tick mark near the bottom-right corner of their image, indicating that these Apps are downloaded and installed on the Kindle Fire.

If you touch and hold an App on the **Cloud** that is not already on your **Device**, you are given the option to add it to your **Device**. However, if such an App is already on your **Device** and you touch and hold it, you are given the option to remove it from your **Device**.

The Settings Screen

There are two ways you can use to display the device settings screen:

(a) Tap the **Home**  button to return your Kindle Fire to its **Home** screen (the one showing the **Carousel**), then tap the **Apps library** link to open the screen shown in Fig. 2.14.

Fig. 2.14 The Starting and Installed Apps Screen.

Note the pre-installed **Settings** Apps on this screen. Tapping it, displays the **Settings** screen shown in Fig. 2.16 on the next page.

(b) Place your stylus (or your finger) next to the time at the top of the screen and swipe downwards to reveal the **Device Control Screen**, as shown in Fig. 2.15 on the next page.

Fig. 2.15 The Device Control Screen.

Again, note the **Settings** option on the above **Device Control** screen. You can also use this screen to control some of your device's functions, such as **Auto-Rotation**, the **Brightness** of its screen, the **Wireless** connection, **Quiet Time** and **Mayday**.

Tapping the **Settings** option displays the same full set of **Settings** which control your device, including running **Applications**, **Parental Controls**, **Wireless** connection **Accessibility** and a lot more besides, as shown in Fig. 2.16.

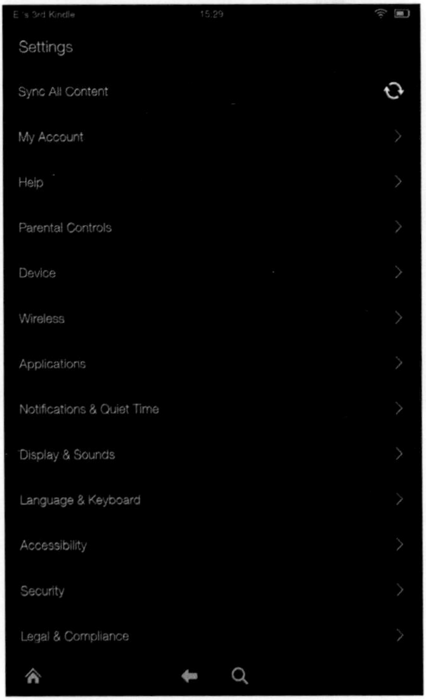

Fig. 2.16 The Settings Screen.

I shall return to the **Settings** screen later on in the book when it is needed, but while you are here, you might like to tap the **Applications** entry and turn **On** the **Apps from Unknown Sources** option on the displayed screen, as shown in Fig. 2.17.

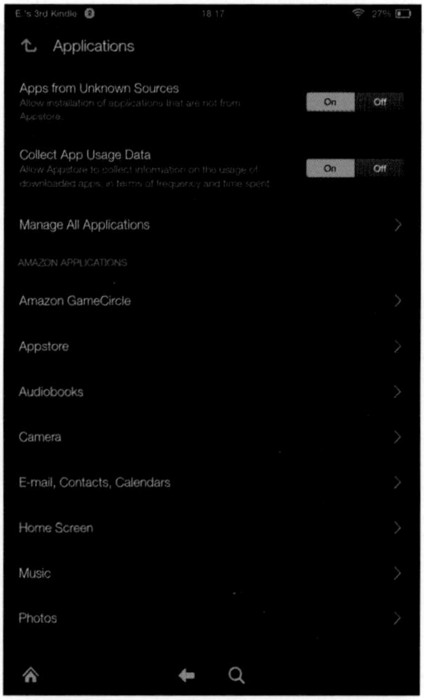

Fig. 2.17 The Applications Settings Screen.

Doing so, you'll get a stern warning, as shown in Fig. 2.18, but you may ignore it if you wish to continue!.

Fig. 2.18 Warning Against Using Non-Amazon Apps.

The Mayday Facility

The **Mayday** facility, shown here, can be accessed from the **Device Control Screen** (see Fig. 2.15, page 24). Tapping this option, displays the screen in Fig. 2.19.

Fig. 2.19 The Mayday Facility Screen.

This Facility provides a 24/7 direct support for the Kindle Fire HDX. It gives you access to a video-based support connection to a Kindle expert who can respond to your queries with actual answers. The expert can take over your screen, draw on it to show you where a needed control is, until you understand what you have to do to solve your problem. However, you must be on line.

The **Mayday** facility is a tremendous innovation on the part of Amazon who give their customers first priority. A very worthwhile facility to try for yourself!

3

Web Browsing & Printing

You can use the Kindle Fire built-in **Silk** App to explore the Web, or you can download a different Web browser.

Exploring the Web With Silk

Kindle Fire provides the **Silk** App so you can explore the Web. First tap the **Home** 🏠 button to return your Kindle Fire to its **Home** screen (the one showing the **Carousel**), then tap the **Apps library** link to open the screen shown in Fig. 3.1.

Fig. 3.1 The Starting Apps Screen.

 Now tapping the **Silk** App icon, also shown here, then follow by tapping the **New Tab** ➕ icon that is to be found at the top-right of the newly opened **Silk** screen, which displays the screen in Fig. 3.2 on the next page. If you don't tap the **New Tab** ➕ icon, what displays on your screen is the last Web page you happen to be looking at in the **Silk** browser.

Fig. 3.2 The New Tab Screen in Silk.

The same screen can also be displayed by tapping the **Web library** link, followed by **New tab** on the **Home** screen.

The above screen displays the **Most Visited** Web sites, if indeed you have looked at any. Additional options can be seen by tapping the **Options** ☰ button at the top-left of the above screen. Apart from the **Most Visited** link, you'll see links to **Bookmarks**, **Downloads**, **History** and **Trending Now**. It is worth looking at these to find out what is offered. I will discuss **Bookmarks** and **Downloads** shortly.

The Address Bar

In **Silk**, the **Address bar** is where you type, or paste the address or URL (Uniform Resource Locator) of a Web page you want to open. For example, type in the **Address bar** what is shown in Fig. 3.3 on the next page.

Fig. 3.3 The Address Bar.

This displays what is shown above, below the **Address bar**, if you have visited that Web site before. Selecting the first option with **http://** in front of the address, opens my personal Web page when the **Go** button on the on-screen keyboard is tapped, while selecting the second option, searched the Web for the occurrence of the name.

Note that once the Web page is opened, a **Refresh** ↻ button is displayed at the far right of the **Address bar** replacing the **Cancel** ⊠ button.

The **Address bar** is the main way of opening new Web pages when you know their URLs, but having opened one such page, tapping the **Silk** explorer icon or the **Web library** link displays the same previously opened Web page, unless you first close such a page by tapping the **Close** ⊠ button on the Web page's tab (see Fig. 3.4 below), in which case tapping either the **Silk** icon or the **Web library** link, displays the **New Ta**b screen (see Fig. 3.2 on the previous page).

Fig. 3.4 The Opened Web Page's Tab.

Tabbed Browsing

With tabbed browsing you can open several Web sites in one **Silk** window each in its own tab, and switch between them by tapping on their tab. To create a new tab, tap the **New tab** ⊞ icon to be found to the far right of the existing tabs (Fig. 3.4).

As an example, try to open the **Google** page as an additional Web page to one you have opened already. In my case, the displayed screen is shown in Fig. 3.5 below.

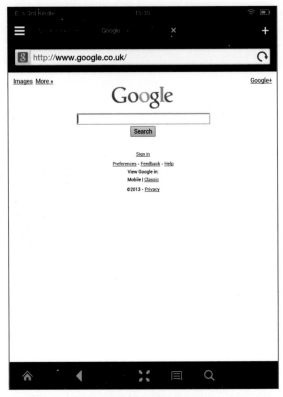

Fig. 3.5 A Tabbed Silk Screen.

Note: Immediately to the left of the **View** button in Fig. 3.5 above is the **Full Screen** ✖ button. Tapping this button displays the contents of your screen in full screen mode with a compressed **View** ▬ button appearing at the bottom of the screen. Tapping this button returns you to normal view.

While on a Web site, if you tap the **View** 🖩 button an extended **View** menu appears on your screen, as shown in Fig. 3.6, where I only show the bottom half of the screen.

Fig. 3.6 The Extended View Menu when Looking at a Web Site.

From the above **View** menu you could go to the **Share Page**

option which displays a **Share To** menu, as shown in Fig. 3.7. This menu includes sharing options via **E-mail** (the subject of Chapter 4), via **Facebook** or **Twitter**. The other important **Share To** option is the ability to **Print** to an 'Air Printer' (WiFi connected).

Fig. 3.7 The Share Options Menu.

Search Engines

If you know the URL of a Web page, you can type it in the address bar of your browser. But if you are just looking for something specific, like heritage places to visit, then you need a search engine, one of which is **Google**, the world's most popular. Kindle Fire HDX uses **bing** (a Microsoft product) as its default search engine.

To use all the facilities available in **Google**, like **Google Chrome** (an alternative to **Silk**) or **Gmail** (to be discussed shortly), you need to be registered with **Google**. Obviously it is up to you whether you continue to use **bing** or start using the **Google** search engine instead. Using **Google** as a search engine does not require registration.

Bookmarks and History

To add a **Bookmark**, first search for the Web site you want to

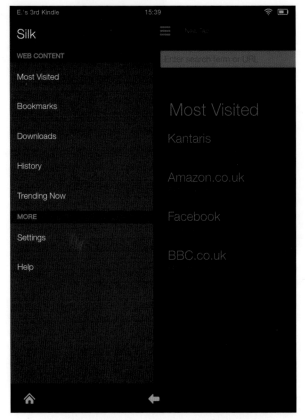

bookmark, say **Amazon's** UK site, search the site for the required Web page, then tap the **Options** icon shown here which is located in the top left of the screen above the **Address bar**. This opens the **Options** screen shown in Fig. 3.8 below.

Fig. 3.8 The Web Options Screen.

Next, tap the **Bookmarks** entry on the displayed screen to open the screen shown in Fig. 3.9 on the next page.

Fig. 3.9 The Bookmarks Screen.

As you can see, **Google** is already in my **Bookmarks**. Now tap the **Add** button to display the screen in Fig. 3.10.

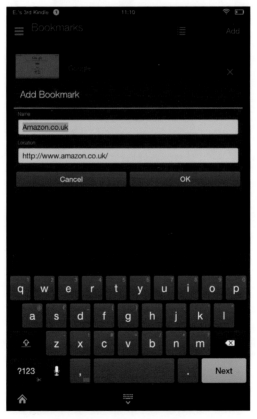

Fig. 3.10 Creating a Bookmark.

Next time you visit **Bookmarks** you'll see the newly created bookmark listed in **Tile** view (top of Fig. 3.11). Tapping the **List** view button displays the bottom part of the same figure.

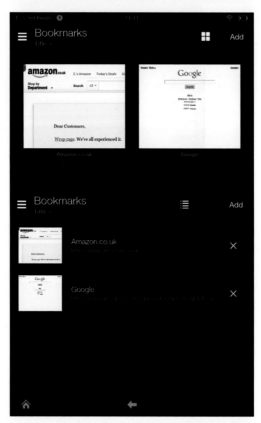

Fig. 3.11 The Bookmarks Screen.

To delete **Bookmarks**, either touch and hold a bookmark in the **Tile View** and select **Delete** from the displayed contextual menu, or tap the **List View** button and on the displayed screen (bottom of Fig. 3.11), tap the ⊠ button.

Bookmarks make it a lot easier and faster to locate a frequently visited Web page.

Next, return to the **Web Options** screen (Fig. 3.8, page 32) and tap the **History** option to display a screen similar to that in Fig. 3.12 below.

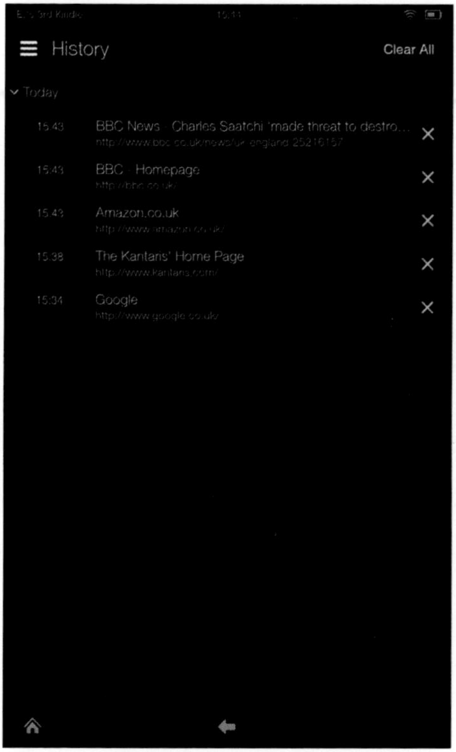

Fig. 3.12 The History Screen.

In this list you can see what Web sites I visited **Today**. You can also see what was visited **Yesterday**, Last 7 days or **Last month**. If these lists get out of hand, you could **Clear All** of them at a tap of a button, not just the section you were looking at. So be careful when you choose to delete **History**! You do get a warning though.

Tapping a listed site opens links to the individual Web pages you visited in the past. Tapping any of these will open the page again.

The Web Settings Screen

Finally, return to the **Web Options** screen (Fig. 3.8, page 32) and tap the **Settings** entry option to display the screen shown in Fig. 3.13.

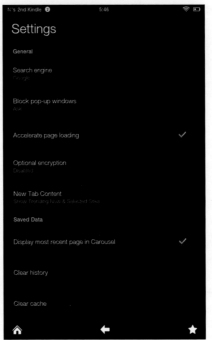

Fig. 3.13 The Web Settings Screen.

The **Web Settings** list is almost two times longer than that displayed in Fig. 3.13. To see the rest of the entries, scroll upwards. I'll discuss some of these settings as and when I need to, as they control your interaction with the Web.

While on the **Web Settings** screen you might like to change the search engine the Kindle is using. Tapping the first option under **General** displays three options to choose from: **bing**, **Google** or **Yahoo! UK & Ireland**. The choice is yours to make!

The Device Settings Screen

To display the **Device Applications** screen, first tap the **Home** icon, then swipe from the edge of the Kindle that displays the time towards the middle of the screen to display the **Device Control Screen** (see page 24 in the previous chapter), also shown here in Fig. 3.14.

Fig. 3.14 The Device Control Screen.

Tapping the **Settings** button followed by the **Device** entry, displays the **Device Settings** screen shown in Fig. 3.15.

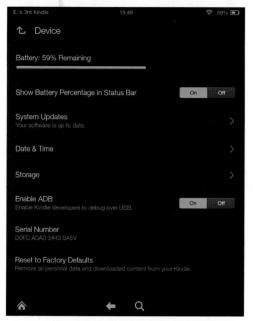

Fig. 3.15 Device Settings Screen.

To display the remaining percentage charge of the battery next to its image at the top right of the screen, turn it **On** as shown above – a helpful visual aid to the state of the battery.

Printing Web Pages, Photos & Files

I am sure that by now you must have asked yourself the question "how do I print from my Kindle Fire?" The answer is "quite simple if you have an e-Printer (WiFi capable), but impossible (at present) if you don't"! Kindle Fire is not supported by **Google Play** which is essential for installing **Chrome** and any Apps that allow printing to non-WiFi printers.

Free Printing to an HP e-Printer

To print to an HP e-printer, you need to download a special **HP** App, called **ePrint which is absolutely free.** To do this, tap **Home**, then **Apps**, then **Store** and search for **eprint**. The result is shown in Fig. 3.16.

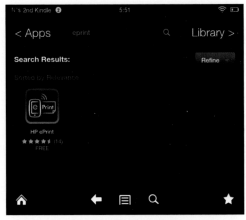

Fig. 3.16 The Free ePrint App.

After buying this App from Amazon for £0.00 (it is free), return to **Home**, tap the **Apps library** link and select **Cloud**. Next, tap and hold the App and select **Download** on the displayed menu. The App is now downloaded on to your **Device**.

Tapping the App on **Device**, displays a screen which tells you what can be achieved with its use.

Finally, a search for the printer starts and a few seconds later it is found as shown in Fig. 3.17, provided the printer is switched on and connected to the Internet. It is as simple as that.

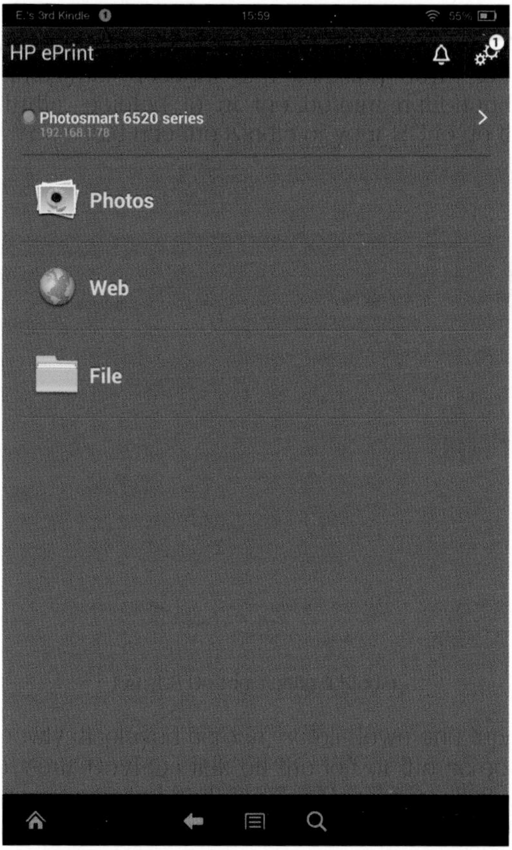

Fig. 3.17 The Recognised HP Wireless Printer and its Capabilities.

With such a printer you can print photos, Web pages and any type of document, such as text files, pdf files or **Word** files.

Printing to Any WiFi Capable Printer

There is an excellent App on the App Store called **StarPrint** which is free to try, as shown in Figure 3.18.

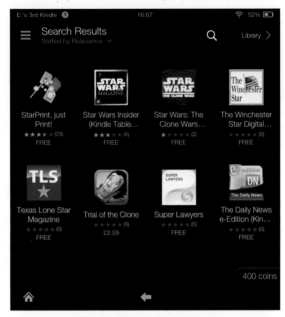

Fig. 3.18 The StarPrint App.

Having purchased it, tapping it installs it on your device and lets you print preview and print on many different WiFi capable printers, but with a watermark.

To remove the watermark you must make a payment of £3.29 for **Photos** and £2.50 for the **Office Pack**. Although this App is not exactly free, it performs extremely well with my HP wireless Printer and the tutorial video advertising its capabilities clearly states that it can print to an **Epson** and a **Canon** printer equally well, a claim I cannot check. I suggest you try this App and test print with the watermark on your own printer before purchasing, as it is easy to install and configure.

4

Keeping in Touch

You can use the built-in **Mail** App of Kindle Fire to send and receive e-mail messages, but you must first configure it. You can use either Web based mail or a POP/IMAP account.

The Kindle E-mail App

 When you first tap the Kindle **Mail** App, shown here, a similar screen to that in Fig. 4.1 displays.

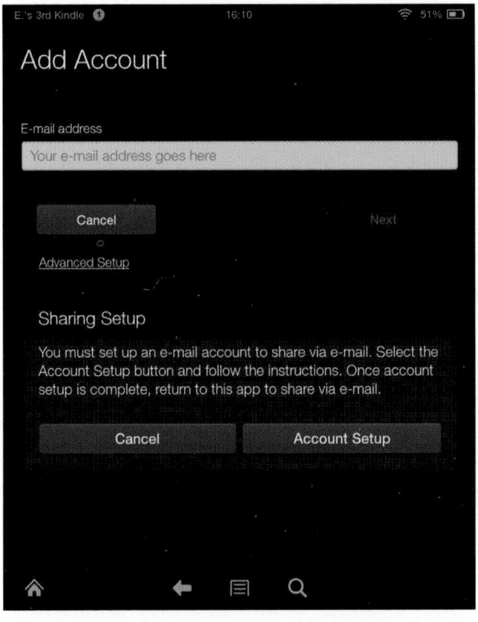

Fig. 4.1 Adding an E-mail Account.

If you already have a Web-based e-mail account, just enter your e-mail address and tap the **Account Setup** button, then follow the on-screen instructions. Web-based accounts are those that you open with **Gmail**, **Hotmail**, **Yahoo**, etc. However, you need to know your account details. I'll discuss one of these shortly.

If, however, your e-mail account is not Web-based, then you should tap the **Advanced Setup** link at the bottom of the list in Fig. 4.1. This displays a series of screens that allow you to insert the details for industry-standard **POP3**, **IMAP** or **Exchange** e-mail accounts. The last of these is normally only used by large corporations.

Configuring a Web-based Account

As an example I'll discuss how you can sign on to Google so that you can get a **Google Mail** (**Gmail** for short) account which is a Web-based application that allows you to create, send and receive e-mail messages using the **Mail** App on the Kindle Fire or using a computer's browser. E-mail messages are stored freely and securely on Google's data sites, so that they are accessible to you at any time from anywhere.

Advantages of Gmail

As **Gmail** is designed around Google's search technology and its vast storage capability, it is easy to:

- Search your e-mail messages to find exactly what you want quickly and efficiently provided you archive rather than delete them. Google provides more than 10.25 GB of storage for your e-mail messages.

- Filter all messages for spam so you don't have to worry about them. If a spam e-mail happens to get through, all you have to do is mark it and delete it.

All Google services, including **Gmail**, are free to you because Google creates enough revenue from 'contextual ads' that (normally) appear to the right of Google search results.

Signing Up to a Google Account

Signing up to Google is required if you hope to use Kindle's **Mail** App or any other Google programs when using your tablet. To start the procedure, open your browser and type:

https://accounts.google.com/signup

in the address bar, then tap **Go** on the on-screen keyboard to display Fig. 4.2 below.

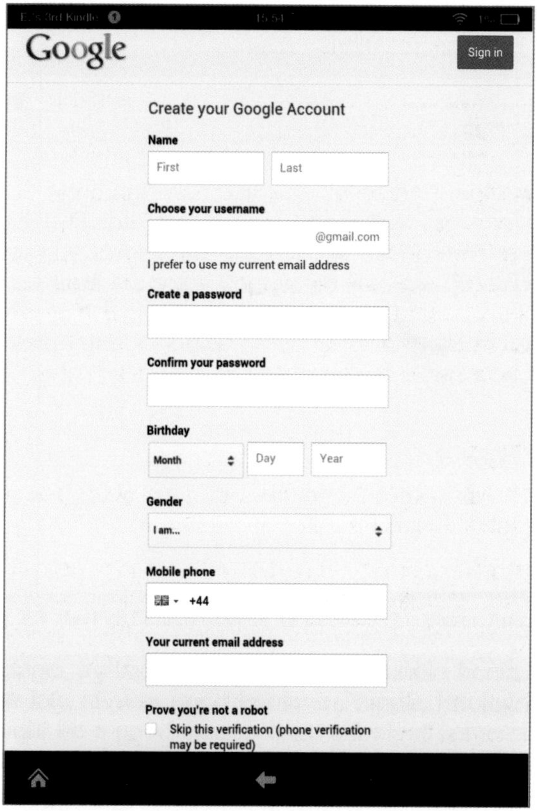

Fig. 4.2 The Create Your Google Account Screen.

You'll have to scroll down to see and enter additional information, such as 'Security questions', 'Secondary e-mail address' (in case you forget your password so it can be sent to you), 'Location' and 'Word verification'. Once these are supplied your account with Google is generated.

 Next, tapping on Kindle's **Mail** App, and signing into **Gmail** with the account details you have just created, displays messages from the **Gmail Team**, similar to those shown in Fig. 4.3 below. Like everything else from Google such content changes often!

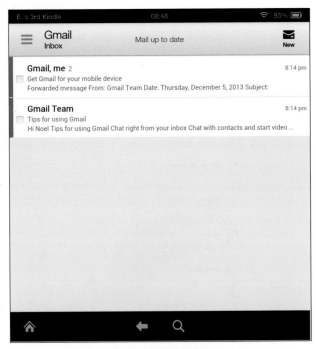

Fig. 4.3 The Gmail Team's Messages.

It is worth spending some time reading what they have to offer in the messages **Get Gmail for your mobile device** and **Tips for using Gmail**.

The Mail App Screen

The **Mail** App screen, displaying the first received e-mail message from the **Gmail Team**, is shown in Fig. 4.3 on the previous page. As you can see, there is an **Options** button to the left of the **Gmail Inbox** at the top left of the screen and an additional **New** button at the top right of the screen.

The Mail App Folders

 Tapping the **Options** button, displays a screen similar to that in Fig. 4.4 with the **Show labels** button activated – once activated it changes to **Hide labels** as shown below. It is best to view such a screen in landscape orientation, otherwise the e-mail messages display truncated.

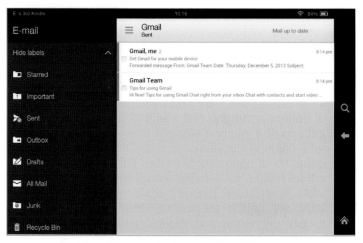

Fig. 4.4 The Gmail Inbox and Other Folders.

The various folders hold the following information:

Drafts – A list of messages you have not sent yet. These are saved in **Drafts**, for you to edit or send.

Outbox – The message you are about to send is momentarily held here before transmission takes place.

Sent – A list of messages you have sent.

Recycle Bin – All the e-mail messages you have deleted. Having looked at these, you can select them (by tapping on the square to the left of each message) and you are then given the option to **Delete** them, **Move** them into another folder or **Mark** them as **Unread** or **Star** them. Deleting messages from the **Recycle Bin**, deletes them permanently.

Junk – All e-mail messages that have been marked as **Junk**.

[Gmail] – (not shown in Fig. 4.4) has sub-folders, such as **All Mail**, where all the messages you have received, sent, or archived are kept, but not those you have deleted.

There are also folders that can hold messages you have **Starred** or categorised as **Important**. The reason for all these folders is because the **Mail** App does not give you the ability to create new folders when you need them, so Amazon has anticipated what you might need!

Tapping the **Options** (or **Gmail Inbox**) once more, closes down the folders list and returns you to your e-mail messages in full-screen – in other words, it acts as a toggle switch.

I shall be discussing these options shortly, but first let us examine the effect of tapping the **New** button in Fig. 4.3 shown on page 44.

The New E-mail Button

Tapping the **New** button, shown here, displays a new e-mail form for you to fill-in (the top-half of which is shown in Fig. 4.5 on the next page. At this point you'll have to type the recipient's e-mail address in the **To:** field. Also, tapping the **Cc/Bcc** link to the right of the **To:** field, displays two additional fields below the **To:** field, namely the **Cc:** and **Bcc:** fields. In all three fields you type e-mail addresses of people to whom you are sending your e-mail.

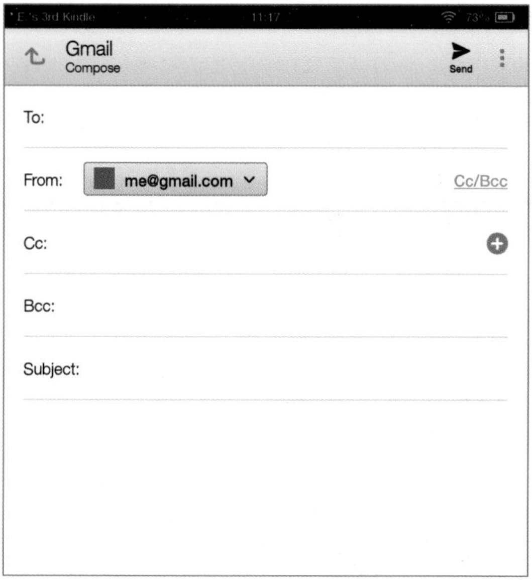

Fig. 4.5 The New Message Screen.

Anyone listed in the **Cc:** field of a message receives a copy of that message when you send it. All other recipients of that message can see that the person(s) you designated as a 'carbon copy' recipient(s), received a copy of the message.

Bcc: stands for 'blind carbon copy'. **Bcc:** recipients are invisible to all other recipients of the message (including other **Bcc:** recipients).

However, e-mail addresses can be quite lengthy, difficult to remember and any mistake you make when typing an address can be quite fatal – not that disastrous really, but simply it will be returned to you marked as undeliverable.

There is, however, a better method of entering e-mail addresses into the various message fields. The method involves the use of the **Contacts** App, which is discussed next.

The Contacts App

You can use the **Contacts** App to make and store a list of all your contacts' names, addresses, phone numbers, e-mail addresses and notes as shown in Fig. 4.6 below.

Fig. 4.6 Creating a New Contact.

Importing a Contacts List

Gmail allows you to import your **Contacts** list from several e-mail programs, such as **Yahoo!**, **Hotmail**, **Outlook** and others. So if you already have a list of contacts on your PC, it would be much easier to import these to your Kindle Fire, rather than having to create each contact individually.

If your version of **Outlook** supports exporting contacts to **.vcf** format, then all is well (in earlier versions of **Outlook** this is done from the **File** menu option). If this is the case, skip the procedure detailed below of sending selected contacts to yourself by e-mail.

However, in **Outlook 2010** and **2013** you can only export to comma separated format which is not what the Kindle Fire expects. So, for the latest versions of **Outlook**, do the following:

- Start **Outlook** on your PC, go to **Contacts**, change the **Current View** to **Card**.

- Select as many of your contacts as you want and forward them to yourself as **Business Cards**.

- On receiving the e-mail, save all attachments to a folder, say **TempContacts**, on your C:\ drive.

Now the contacts you want to transfer to the Kindle Fire **Contacts** App are on your PC, as shown on the left portion of Fig. 4.7 on the next page.

- Connect your Kindle Fire to your PC with the USB cable (supplied with your Kindle) and select to **Open device to view files** when it appears on your screen.

- Drag the **TempContacts** folder from your PC to the Kindle. The result of this action is shown on the right of Fig. 4.7 which is displayed on the next page.

Obviously, if you were able to export your **Contacts** directly to a **.vcf** format, then you drag that file to your Kindle instead.

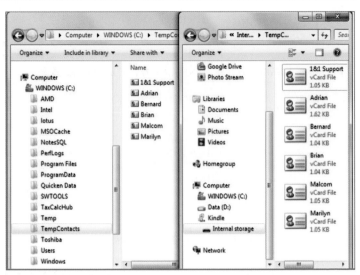

Fig. 4.7 Copying Contacts from PC to Kindle Fire.

To preserve anonymity, I have removed all surnames on the above screens. Next, tap the **Contacts** App on your Kindle Fire, then tap the **Menu** button at the top right of the screen, shown here, then select **Import/Export** on the displayed screen shown in Fig. 4.8.

On the next displayed screen, tap the **Import from Storage** entry and on the subsequent screen choose to **Import all vCard files**. And that's it – as easy as that! All your contacts from **Outlook** are now in your **Contacts** App.

The e-mail addresses of new people who send you a message are added automatically into your **Contacts** if you reply to their message.

Editing a Contact

To edit a contact, perhaps because you want to include additional information or change an e-mail address, simply tap on the contact to open the screen shown in Fig. 4.9.

Fig. 4.9 Opening a Contact in Landscape Orientation.

From here you can **Edit**, **Delete** or add a **New** contact. If you happen to hold your Kindle in portrait orientation, the **Delete** option is not visible. Now tapping the **Edit** button displays the details currently held for the selected contact. Scrolling to the very bottom of the displayed form, you'll see the **Add More Fields** button. Tapping it, displays the screen below.

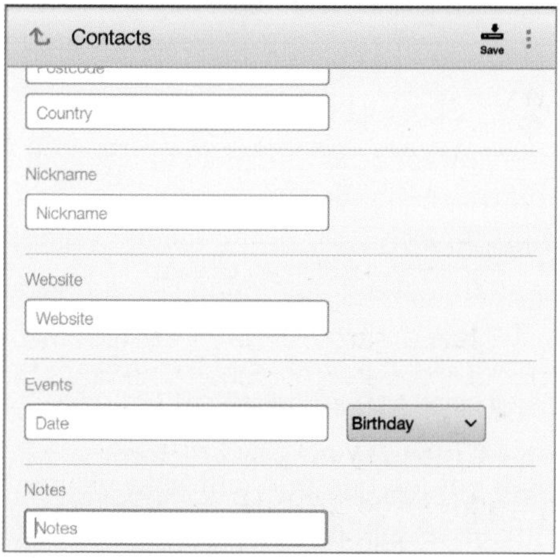

Fig. 4.10 Adding Additional Information to a Contact.

Creating a New Message

When your **Contacts** are sufficiently established, creating and sending a new message is very easy. Tapping the **New** button on the **Mail** App displays the screen in Fig. 4.11.

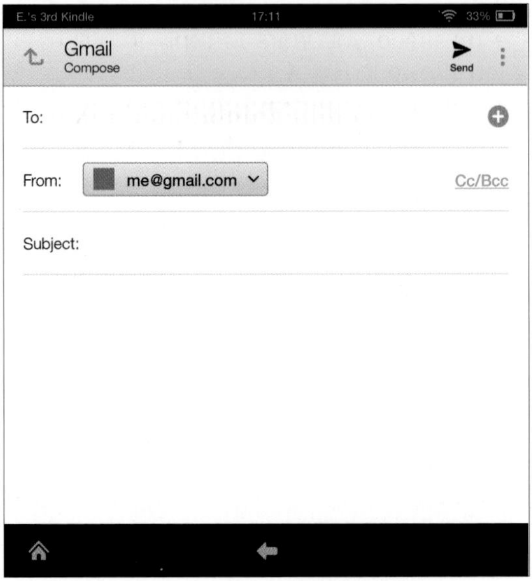

Fig. 4.11 The New Mail Screen.

Now typing the first letter of a recipients name in the **To:** field will list all addresses starting with that letter that are in your **Contacts**. All you have to do is choose the appropriate one.

The best way to test out any unfamiliar e-mail features is to send a test message to your own e-mail address. This saves wasting somebody else's time, and the message can be very quickly checked to see the results.

The text in the **Subject:** field will form a header for the message when it is received, so it helps to show in a few words what the message is about. Finally, type your message and click the **Send** ➤ button.

Replying to a Message

When you receive an e-mail message that you want to reply to, **Mail** makes it very easy to do. The reply address and the new message subject fields are both added automatically for you. Also, by default, the original message is quoted in the reply window.

With the message you want to reply to still open, tap the **Reply** button shown in Fig. 4.12.

Fig. 4.12 Replying to a Message.

As you can see, you can **Reply** to the person who sent you the message, or use the **Reply All** if the message was sent to several people, allowing you to reach all the people who received the message. The **Forward** option is used to send the message to a different person altogether, but you'll have to supply their e-mail address (perhaps from your **Contacts**).

Using E-mail Attachments

Having selected a recipient for a new e-mail, to add an attachment to the e-mail, such as a photo or work file, simply

 tap the **Menu** button shown here and select **Attach Photo** or **Attach File** from the drop-down options screen shown in Fig. 4.13.

You can now browse what is available on your computer to find the item you want to attach, including your libraries where you might have saved documents or pictures. Below, selected photos in my **Photos library** are shown after attaching them to the message.

Your e-mail should now look similar to the one shown in Fig. 4.13 below.

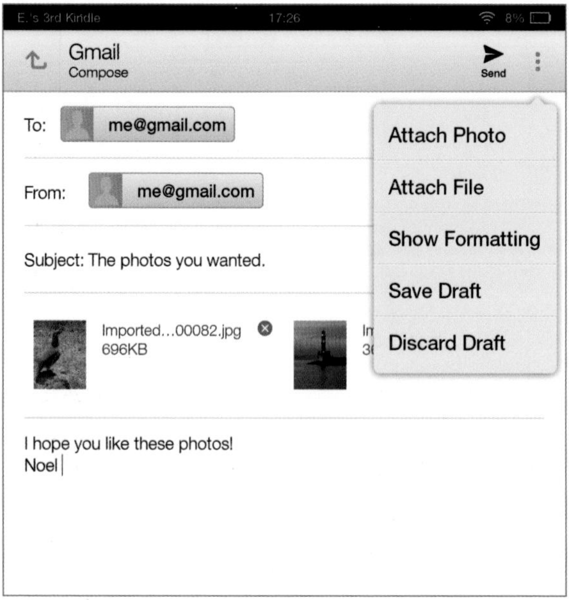

Fig. 4.13 An E-mail Message with Attached Photos.

All you have to do now is send the e-mail, perhaps to yourself, so you can see and check the result.

Receiving Attachments

Fig. 4.14 below shows the e-mail you'll receive with its attachments had you sent it to yourself.

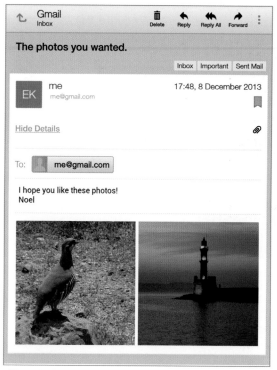

Fig. 4.14 Received E-mail Message with Attached Photos.

Touching and holding a picture displays their name (if already named) and type (for example **.jpg**) and you are invited to **Open** or **Save** them as shown in Fig. 4.15.

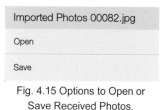

Fig. 4.15 Options to Open or Save Received Photos.

If you choose the **Open** option, the picture will be displayed in full screen while selecting to **Save** it, it will be saved in your **Photos library**.

Deleting Messages

Some e-mail messages you receive will be worth keeping, but most will need deleting. With an e-mail opened, just tap the **Delete** 🗑 button to complete the action. Deleted e-mail messages are placed in the **Recycle Bin**. You can find the **Recycle Bin** by tapping the **Options** ≡ button, then selecting the **Show labels** option shown in Fig. 4.16.

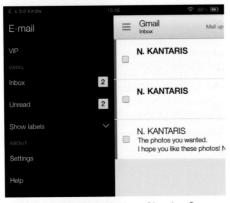

This reveals all the available folders in **Mail**, one of which is the **Recycle Bin**. If ignored, this folder gets bigger and bigger over time, so you need to check it from time to time manually and re-delete messages you will not need again. If you deleted a message by mistake, you can

Fig. 4.16 The Menu Options Showing Some Folders.

move it back to the **Inbox** (or another folder) by tapping the **Move** button shown in Fig. 4.17.

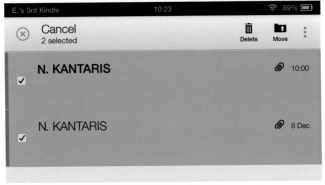

Fig. 4.17 Moving a Message.

The Calendar App

The **Calendar** is the diary and scheduling App of Kindle Fire in which you can create and manage appointments, meetings and events. But before starting to enter information in **Calendar**, let us take a look at its opening screen.

To open **Calendar**, tap the **Calendar** App which displays **Calendar** (first time only) in **Day** view. You can choose to display **Calendar** in several views; **List**, **Day**, **Week** and **Month**, as shown here. Having chosen one of these, **Calendar** opens in your chosen view next time you access it. Fig. 4.18 below shows **Calendar** in **Month** and **Landscape** view.

	Mon	Tue	Wed	Thu	Fri	Sat	Sun
December 2013							
	25	26	27	28	29	30	1
	2	3	4	5	6	7	8
	9	10	11	12	13	14	15
	16	17	18	19	20	21	22
	23	24	25	26	27	28	29
	30	31	1	2	3	4	5

Fig. 4.18 The Calendar App in Month View.

The Options Menu

Tapping the **Menu** button, displays the available options shown here and tapping the **New Event** option displays the screen shown in Fig. 4.19 on the next page.

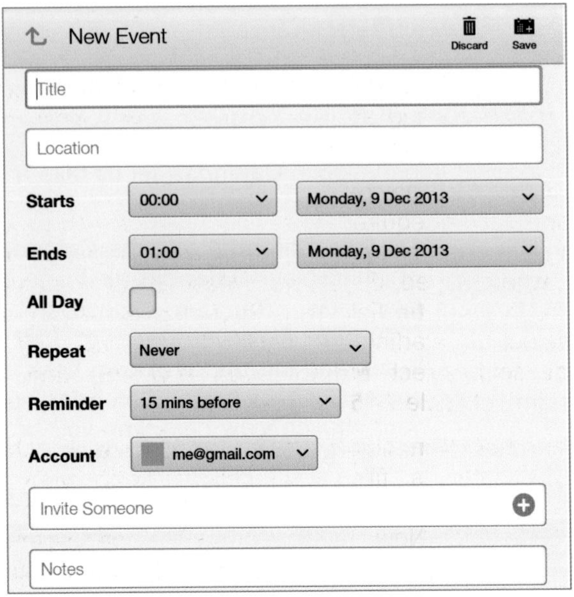
New Event
Discard
Save
Title
Location
Starts
00:00
Monday, 9 Dec 2013
Ends
01:00
Monday, 9 Dec 2013
All Day
Repeat
Never
Reminder
15 mins before
Account
me@gmail.com
Invite Someone
Notes

Fig. 4.19 The Top-half of the New Event Screen.

Use the on-screen keyboard to fill in the displayed **Event** form, remembering that:

- An **All Day** event normally does not involve other people or resources but is an activity that lasts all day, such as attendance at an exhibition or conference.
- An event that requires an **Invite** is normally a meeting that involves other people and possibly resources and can also be recurring. You can choose the length of recurrence by tapping the down-arrow against **Repeat** and selecting one of the options shown in Fig. 4.20.

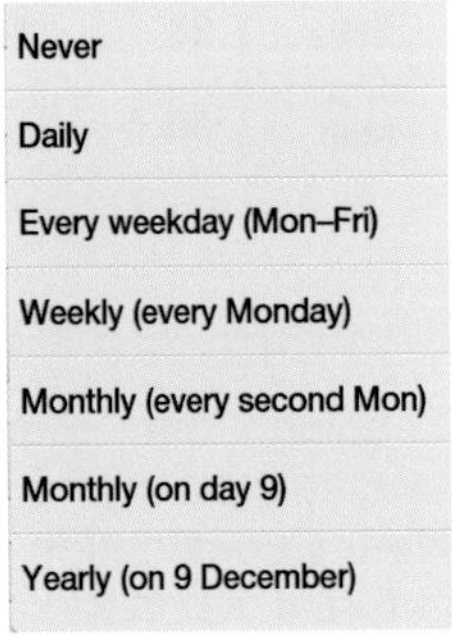
Never
Daily
Every weekday (Mon–Fri)
Weekly (every Monday)
Monthly (every second Mon)
Monthly (on day 9)
Yearly (on 9 December)

Fig. 4.20 Repeat Options.

Creating an Event

As an example let us create a recurring event to, say, meet 'Local Society Members', that takes place on the 16th day of every month starting at 10:00 a.m. on 16th December and lasting for 1 hour.

To create this, navigate to the starting date on a **Month** view and tap the required date. This opens the **Day** view and tapping the 10 a.m. slot you are offered a **New event** icon which, when tapped, displays the **New Event** screen for you to fill in. In the **Title** field type **Society's Monthly Meeting**, then select the starting and ending times if different. In the **Repeat** field select **Monthly (on day 16)** and in the **Reminder** field select **15 minutes before**.

In the **Location** field type **Community Hall**, while the **Account** entry is filled automatically with your e-mail address. Tap the down-arrowhead and change this field to your **Calendar**. Now tapping the ⊕ icon, opens your **Contacts** list for you to select one participant each time you tap the icon.

Fig. 4.21 Arranging a Meeting.

Again, for the sake of anonymity, I have removed the surnames of the invited individuals and tapping the **Save**  button, saves the **Calendar** entry.

The entry on a **Month** view displays underlined to let you know that an event is scheduled for that date, as are other important days (holidays in Fig. 4.18, page 57).

Editing an Event

If you want to edit an event, first tap its entry to open it in **Day** view, as shown in Fig. 4.22, then tap again its **Day** view to open a screen similar to that in Fig. 4.23.

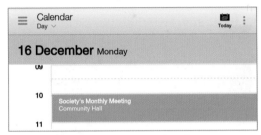

Fig. 4.22 The Calendar Day Entry.

You can use the **Menu** button at the top-right of this last screen to edit the event with a choice to apply such changes to this entry only or the whole series.

Fig. 4.23 The Buttons to Edit or Delete a Calendar Entry.

As it stands now, 15 minutes before the monthly meeting is due to start, a reminder window will open on top of everything else.

That's all there is to it; you should never miss your important dates again, but you must make time to enter them in **Calendar** in the first place. Try it, you'll never regret it!

5

Music, Media & Photography

Using the Music Library App

The stereo speakers on the Kindle Fire HDX come into their own when you listen to music. Start by tapping the **Music library** entry on the **Home** screen of your Kindle Fire which displays the screen in Fig. 5.1 below.

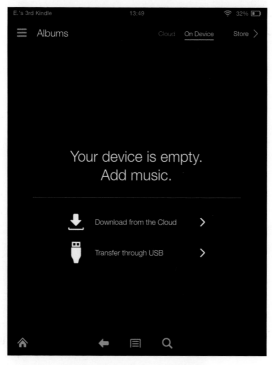

Fig. 5.1 The Music Library App.

Music you buy either from the Amazon store or iTunes is stored on the Amazon cloud (free for the first 250 songs, but after that you'll have to pay! You don't have to download such stored music to your device to listen to it. Instead, you can use Amazon's **MP3 Cloud Player** to enjoy it without having to fill up your Kindle Fire with large files.

To purchase music, tap **Cloud**, then the **Store** link at the top right corner of the screen in Fig. 5.1 shown on the previous page and search for **free** music, which displays a screen similar to that in Fig. 5.2 (only the top-half is shown).

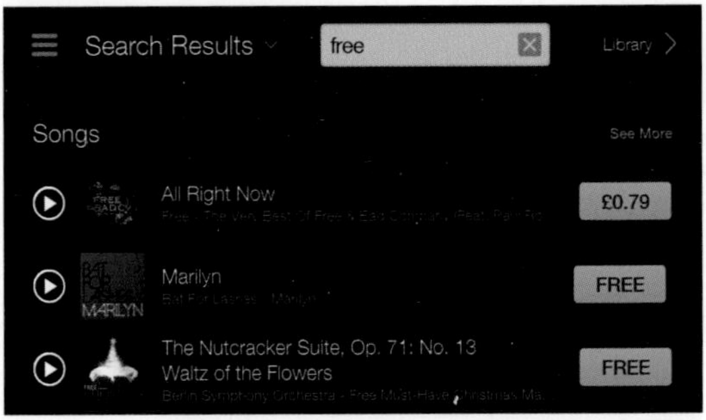

Fig. 5.2 Free Sample Music.

If you tap on one of these, a screen similar to that in Fig. 5.3 is displayed.

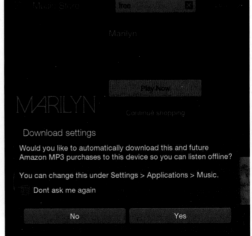

You can listen to the music to see whether you like what you hear before committing to buying. You also have a choice of buying a single track or an album.

Fig. 5.3 Choose Download Settings.

All the music you have already purchased is listed as such. You could also search for any category of music, such as **classical**, **trad jazz**, etc. You'll find plenty of choice.

If, however, you prefer to listen to your own CD collection, then you'll have to transfer your music from your computer to the Kindle Fire.

Transferring Music from Computer to Kindle

To transfer selected music from your computer to the **Music library** on your Kindle Fire, do the following:

- Connect your Kindle to your PC or Mac using the supplied USB cable, then select the **Open device to view files** on the **Autoplay** screen that displays. This shows the Kindle's **Internal Storage**, as shown on the left-top of Fig. 5.4.

- Use the **File Explorer** on your computer to locate the individual music or folder you want to transfer to the Kindle and arrange for the two screens to appear side-by-side as shown below, then open the Kindle's **Internal Storage** and locate the **Music library** folder, then drag your selection from the computer to the **Music library**.

- Unless the music you are transferring to the Kindle Fire is in MP3 format, you'll get a warning screen telling you that such music file will not play on your Kindle Fire, as shown in Fig. 5.4. **Ignore the warning** and press **Yes**.

Fig. 5.4 Transferring Music from PC to Kindle Fire.

Normally CD music which was downloaded to your PC will be in **.wma** (Windows Media Audio) file format and such a file cannot be played on the Kindle Fire, hence the warning, unless you purchase a **File Converter** App.

File Format Converter

There is an excellent **File Format Converter** App in the **App Store**. To find it go to **Home**, tap the **Apps library**, then the **Store** at the top right of the screen and search for **File Format Converter**. Amongst the Apps that display, select the **File Converter** shown in Fig. 5.5 below

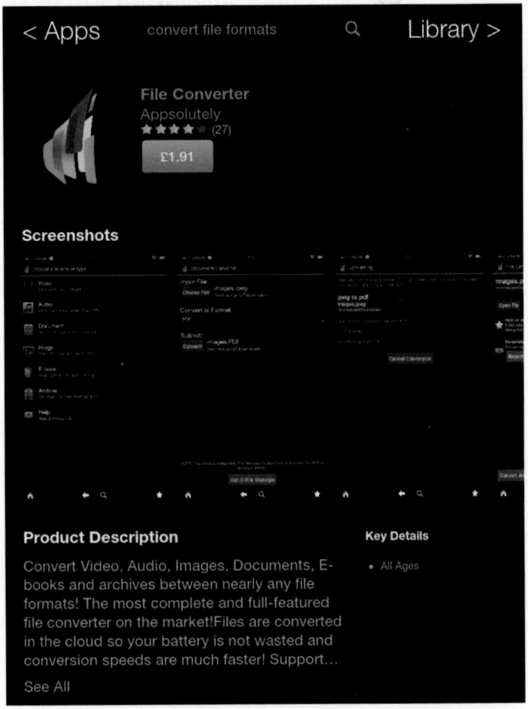

Fig. 5.5 The File Converter App.

After purchasing and installing this App, opening it displays the screen in Fig. 5.6 on the next page.

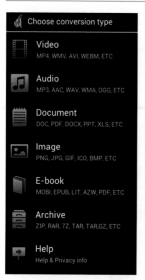

Fig. 5.6 Choosing File Format Conversion Type.

Selecting the **Audio** option displays a screen asking you to choose a file to convert to MP3, as shown in Fig. 5.7. The file to be converted must be on the Kindle Fire. This is why you were advised earlier (Fig. 5.4, page 63) to ignore the warning message when copying music from your PC to the Kindle Fire.

Tapping the **Choose File** button, allows you to navigate first to the Kindle's **Internal Storage**, then to the **Music library** folder.

Next, navigate to the **Music library** folder on your Kindle Fire, select the track you want to convert and tap **Convert** under **Submit**.

There is a limit of 1 GB for any submitted file for conversion, as it takes place on the **File Converter's** server on the cloud. The file is then uploaded, converted and the MP3 file is downloaded to your device within a few seconds, then a screen similar to that shown in Fig. 5.8 on the next page is displayed.

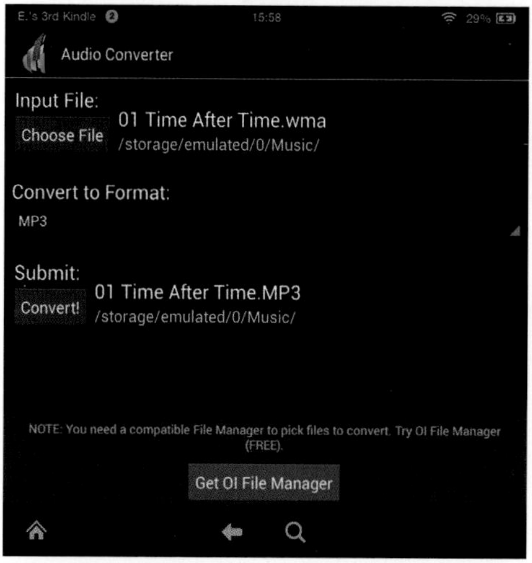

Fig. 5.7 Submitting a File for Conversion.

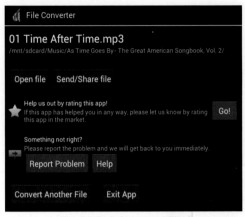

Fig. 5.8 The Converted File.

You can now either play the converted file by tapping the **Open file** button, share it with a friend, report a problem or **Convert Another File**. It might take a bit of time to convert a whole CD, but it is nice to know that you can have your prized music on the Kindle Fire, thanks to the **File Converter**.

Next, using your computer's File Explorer, navigate to the **Music library** folder of Kindle Fire's **Internal Storage** and tap it to display the screen in Fig. 5.9.

Note that there are two files with the same name; one with the extension **.mp3** and the other with the extension **.wma**. You need to delete all the **.wma** files from your Kindle Fire to conserve memory.

If you want to be able to do this operation from your Kindle Fire, then you'll have to download the free **OI File Manager** (see Fig. 5.7).

Fig. 5.9 The Music Files.

Tapping the link provided at the bottom of Fig. 5.7 on page 65, then using the **Appstore** displays what is shown in Fig. 5.10 (only the top-half of the screen is shown).

Fig. 5.10 The Converted File.

The **ES File Explorer** is an excellent file manager and I suggest you download it.

Having done so, you can now use it to delete unwanted files. Tapping a file, selects it and to delete it, tap the **Delete** icon that displays at the bottom of your Kindle's screen.

To find your newly converted files, go to **Home**, then **Music library**, then select **Device** to see all the converted files as shown in Fig. 5.11 for my case.

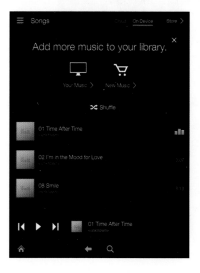

At the bottom of the screen in Fig. 5.11, you'll notice a kind of MP3 music player. You can use this to select a song of your choice and start listening to it.

Music transferred to the Kindle Fire in this way can be played even when not connected to the Internet, which can be very useful.

Fig. 5.11 The Converted Music Songs on Device.

Managing Media

All your media needs are managed by the **IMDb** App which
stands for **Internet Movie Database** that comes
with the Kindle Fire and found on the **Apps library**
of the **Home** screen on the **Cloud**, also shown here.
Tapping this App, displays a screen similar to that in Fig. 5.12
below where the **Options** menu is also activated and
displaying.

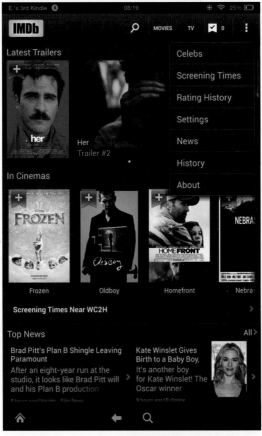

Fig. 5.12 The Internet Movie Database Screen.

Note the three tabs at the top of the screen in Fig. 5.12, namely, **Movies**, **TV** and the ☑ which stands for **Watchlist**.

Using the first tab, you can search the **Internet Movie Database** for specific **Movies**, look at the most viewed titles as some sort of a guide or buy the DVD from Amazon after its release date, if not available now. You can do the same thing with the **TV** tab or you can try the **Celebs** from the **Options** menu. This opens a screen similar to that in Fig. 5.13.

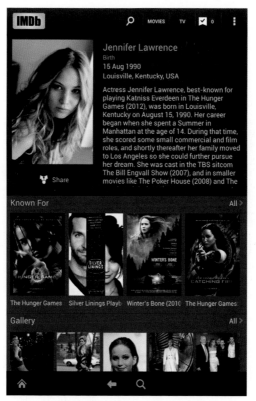

Fig. 5.13 The IMDb's Celebs Screen.

On the **Celebs** screen you can search for your favourite celebrity, and read all about their lives, in which films or TV episodes they acted, etc. I leave it to you to explore these rather time consuming facilities available in the **IMDb** App.

Photography

Under photography, I'll cover both **Photos** and **Videos**, as they are essentially the same. With the Kindle Fire you can use the front facing camera to take photos, but you'll need to download an App to use it as a camcorder.

The Photos Library and the Camera

The Kindle Fire has a **Photos library** which is reached from the **Home** screen. When you access this for the first time, you get three helpful screens informing you what you can do with this App. Photos you take using its camera, photos you saved from e-mail attachments or photos you shared with someone (including those on **Facebook**), will be found here, as shown for my Kindle in Fig. 5.14 below.

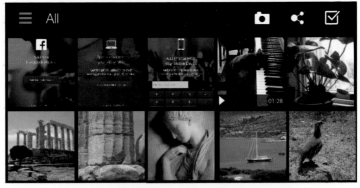

Fig. 5.14 The Photos Library.

The first three photos are the 'helpful' ones you encounter when you first tap the **Photos library**. The next is a video, distinguished by the white right-arrowhead, while the fifth is a photo taken using the Kindle Fire's forward facing camera. Finally, the second row shows photos imported to the Kindle from my camera.

The three buttons at the top-right of Fig. 5.14 shown above, allow you to activate the forward facing camera, share a specified photo or mark a photo with a tick to be printed or deleted.

Using the Camera

When the **Camera** is activated, an image of the shutter of a camera appears at the bottom of the screen, as shown here.

Tapping this image takes a photo of what appears on the Kindle Fire's screen and places it in the small square to the right of the shutter. To take a photo, tilt the Kindle slightly

away from yourself, to make it possible to take a photo of other objects, like the one shown in Fig. 5.15.

Tapping the camera image to the right of the small square, turns the camera to a video recorder, as shown below and tapping the red button starts the video recorder. To stop recording, tap the same button again.

Fig. 5.15 A Photo Taken Using the Kindle Fire's Camera.

Any other photos you take using the Kindle Fire will be placed in the same **Photos library** by default. If you tap the **Share** image (see Fig. 5.14 on the previous page), you'll be told to select a photo (by tapping it), as shown in Fig. 5.16.

Please select the photos you want to share.

Fig. 5.16 About to Select a Photo to Share.

Touching a photo, selects it and you are then able to use the **More** button in Fig. 5.16 to access more choices. Doing so, displays a menu of options for you to choose from, as shown in Fig. 5.17 on the next page.

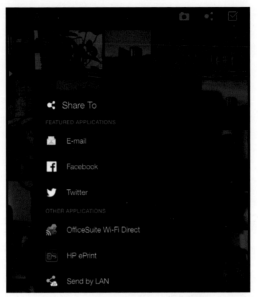

Fig. 5.17 The Share Options Menu List.

You can now send the selected photo by **E-mail** to a friend or upload it to **Facebook** or **Twitter** or even send it to a WiFi connected **Printer**.

Transferring Photos from Computer to Kindle

The transfer of selected photos from your computer to the **Photos library** of your Kindle Fire, follows the same procedure as the one I discussed in detail earlier on page 63 of this chapter when transferring songs to the **Music library**. Follow that procedure, but substitute **Pictures** for **Music**.

The result of dragging your selected photos from the computer to the **Pictures** folder of the Kindle Fire is displayed on the Kindle in the **Photos library** as shown in Fig. 5.18 for my choice on the next page.

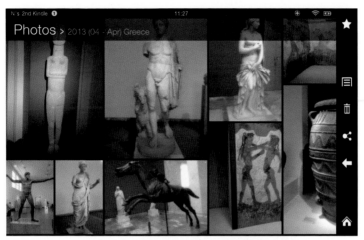

Fig. 5.18 Transferred Photos to Kindle Fire.

Tapping on any one photo within the **Photos library**, displays that photo in full screen. Photos can be removed from your Kindle Fire as explained earlier, but cannot be posted to **Facebook** unless they are first uploaded to the **Cloud**.

Uploading Photos or Videos to the Cloud

To upload photos or videos which reside either on your computer or your Kindle Fire to your Amazon's **Cloud**, you need to download a special App to your **Desktop**. The easiest way of finding this App is to use your Web browser on your computer and search the Internet for:

amazon cloud drive

and select the following from all the search results displayed.

Amazon Cloud Drive - Amazon.co.uk
www.**amazon**.co.uk/gp/feature.html?ie=UTF8&docId=1000655803
Online Storage That Fits Your Life. Never worry about losing a precious memory or not having access to your important files on the go. **Amazon Cloud** Drive ...

As you can see, the address to that Web page is rather complicated, hence the search. Tapping this link displays Fig. 5.19 on the next page.

Fig. 5.19 The Amazon Cloud Drive Apps.

Do note that you only get 5 GB free, after which you'll have to pay. Amazon has only implemented this special App for the PC and the Mac. This means that photos or videos can only be sent to your Amazon's **Cloud** directly, if they are to be found on your PC or Mac, but not on your Kindle Fire!

To start the download of this special App, select the **Desktop app** for a PC or the **Apple Store** for a Mac. Clicking the **Get the Desktop app** in the case of a PC, displays in turn several screens, including a **Sign In** screen, after which the download of the required App starts, creates a **Cloud Drive** for you and displays a screen similar to that shown in Fig. 5.20 below.

Fig. 5.20 Creating the Amazon Cloud Drive.

Note that at present the maximum size of the **Cloud Drive** offered is 119 GB, but only 5 GB of this is free.

Your **Cloud Drive** is then created with three folders as shown in Fig. 5.21 and updated so that everything you had on the **Cloud** can now be found on these folders.

Fig. 5.21 Your Three Folders on Cloud Drive.

The advantage of having your **Documents**, **Pictures** and **Videos** on **Cloud Drive** is that you can access them from any device wherever you are, provided you have Internet connection. However, if you need to refer to any such item off-line, then you must have it on your device.

To complete transfer of items from your PC or Mac or indeed Kindle Fire (as shown below) to an appropriate folder on the **Cloud Drive**, locate what you want to copy and arrange the two screens on your PC or Mac side-by-side as shown in Fig. 5.22 for a PC, then drag the folder or selected items to the **Cloud Drive**.

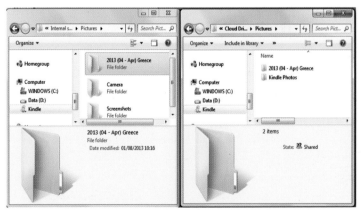

Fig. 5.22 Copying Items to the Cloud Drive.

Items transferred from your PC or Mac to the **Cloud Drive** are automatically transferred to the Kindle Fire HDX and therefore are available to you whether you have Internet connection or not.

Unfortunately the **Video library** on the Kindle is solely taken with Amazon's sales of DVDs of video and TV shows. You cannot include your own videos, even if you copy a video to the **Video** folder on **Cloud Drive**. Such copied videos will be found in the **Photos library** instead and can only be played if you are connected to the Internet.

In contrast, videos taken using your Kindle Fire HDX can be played on it even if you are not connected to the Internet. Pity Amazon has not provided a backward facing camera for the 7" screen model. This facility is only available on the 8.9" model.

6

Kindle Fire Entertainment

You can use your Kindle Fire HDX to listen to the radio while you are reading, watch TV and a lot more besides.

Listening to Radio on the Kindle Fire

There are a lot of Apps you can download and install on the Kindle Fire HDX that allow you to listen to the radio while you are doing something else, like browsing the Internet or perhaps reading a lightweight book!

My favourite App is to be found on Amazon's **Appstore**. To get it, go to the **Home** screen, tap the **Apps library** link, followed by **Store** at the top right of the screen and on the displayed screen search for **radio uk**. Amongst the many Apps offered, I prefer the **Radioplayer** shown in Fig. 6.1. Tap on its icon to buy it – it is free.

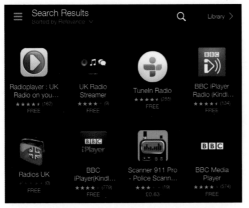

Fig. 6.1 Some of the Radio UK Apps on Offer.

Opening the Radioplayer App

After buying the App and installing it, tap **Open** to display a screen similar to that in Fig. 6.2 below, after tapping **Start listening** on a helpful screen.

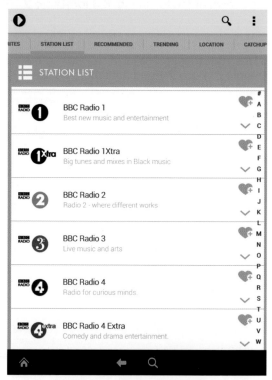

Fig. 6.2 The Radioplayer's Opening Screen.

What I like about this App is twofold: First, it allows you to search for your favourite radio station and after finding it, you can add it to a **Favourites** band, as shown partly in Fig. 6.2 above (you'll have to scroll to the right to reveal it fully).

Radio stations can be added to the **Favourites** band by selecting them (perhaps after a **Search**), then tapping the grey coloured heart shown above to turn it red, as shown here.

The last radio station you have chosen to include in the **Favourites** band, displays first in that band.

The second reason I like this App is that while listening to some music, the presenter's photo and name is displayed on screen, as shown at the top in Fig. 6.3 for **Radio 2**.

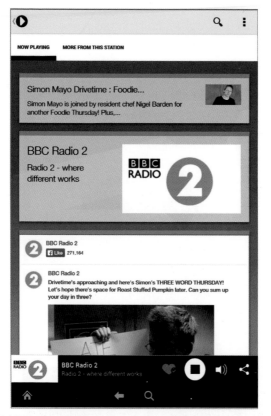

Fig. 6.3 Part of the Radioplayer's Screen While Listening to Radio 2.

To return to your **Favourites**, tap the menu button at the top-left of the screen also shown here. In the case of **Classic FM**, after the display of the presenter's photo, you are also treated to the photo of the composer.

The BBC iPlayer Radio

This is an excellent free App for listening to the BBC radio stations and also catching up on radio programmes that you might have missed. You can find it on Amazon's **Appstore** – see Fig. 6.1 on page 77.

Tap on its icon, shown here, to buy it and install it, then tap **Open**, after installation is complete, to display a screen similar to that shown in Fig. 6.4.

Fig. 6.4 The BBC iPlayer Radio Opening Screen.

The circular carousel at the bottom of the screen displays all the **BBC radio** stations, including local ones, making it easy to change from one to the other.

Catching Up on Missed Radio Programmes

Tapping the menu button at the top of the screen in Fig. 6.4 on the previous page, displays the options shown here to the right. Selecting the last menu option, opens a screen with a full timetable of all the programmes now playing, as well as those on previous days so you can catch up on any missed radio programmes, as shown in Fig. 6.5 below.

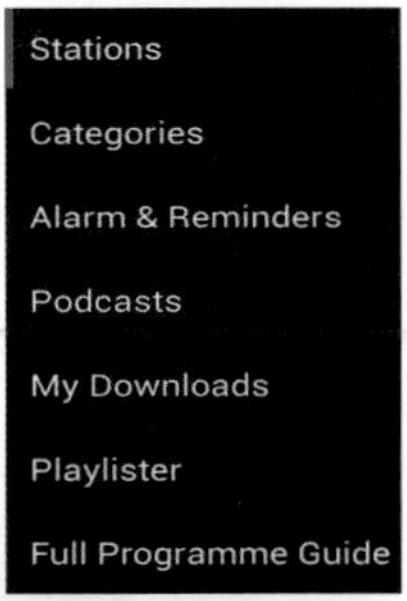

| Stations |
| Categories |
| Alarm & Reminders |
| Podcasts |
| My Downloads |
| Playlister |
| Full Programme Guide |

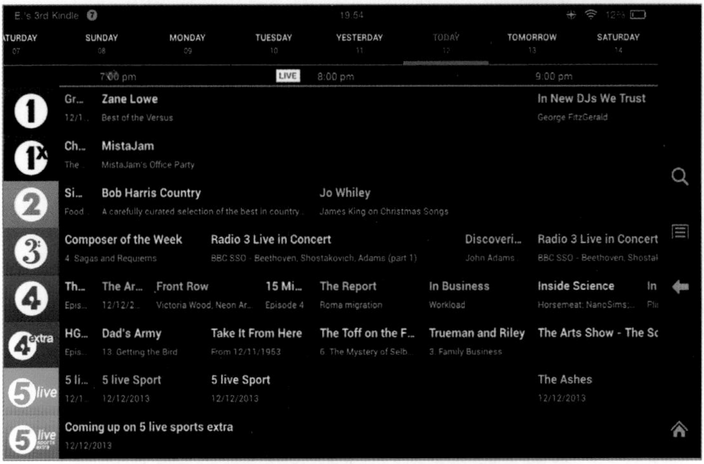

Fig. 6.5 The BBC iPlayer Radio Timetable.

I leave it to you to explore this extremely useful App. Try it, you might find it enjoyable!

Watching TV on the Kindle Fire HDX

To watch TV, get the appropriate App by searching Amazon's **Appstore** for **watch tv**. This returns an enormous number of Apps, which makes it difficult to choose from as some, although recommended with excellent credentials, are only reviewed by a single user!

One of my favourite free Apps for watching TV is the **BBC iPlayer (Kindle Tablet Edition)** shown here. Tap on its icon to buy it and install it, then tap **Open**, after installation is complete. Choosing a program to watch, displays a screen similar to that shown in Fig. 6.6.

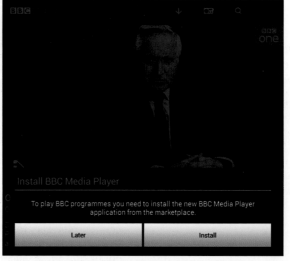

Fig. 6.6 Part of BBC iPlayer's Opening Screen.

To install the new **BBC Media Player**, you must get it via the **Appstore**. You can then choose any program you want to watch. Opening the **BBC Media Player**, you'll see (as indeed is to be expected) that only the **BBC** channels are available.

At the top of the displayed screen you have a choice of three categories: **Featured**, **Most Popular** or **Channels**, as shown in Fig. 6.7. Tapping **Channels**, displays the available **BBC** channels. I leave this to you to experiment with this App.

Fig. 6.7 The BBC iPlayer's Channels.

Note: Do remember that you need a TV licence if you were to watch TV on your Kindle Fire. One licence per household is normally acceptable.

Seeing Additional TV Channels

To see more British TV from both the BBC and other **Freeview** channels, as well as live broadcasts from a score of other countries (from wherever you are), you need to download the free **FilmOn TV** App shown here.

The App creates revenue through adverts which, however, can be skipped. I find these ads unobtrusive, as they are only shown when the App is first started and it only takes a single tap to skip them, but if you find this annoying, you are given the chance to subscribe and skip them automatically.

After installation, tapping the **Open** button displays a screen similar to that in Fig. 6.8. Here you'll find channels specialising in various areas, such as **Sport**, **News**, **Comedy**, **Documentaries**, etc., as well as TV from several countries such as the UK, Germany, Italy, France and even Russia and Australia.

Fig. 6.8 The FilmOn TV's Opening Screen.

Tapping the **UK Live TV** entry and selecting the **Yesterday** channel, displays the screen in Fig. 6.9 below.

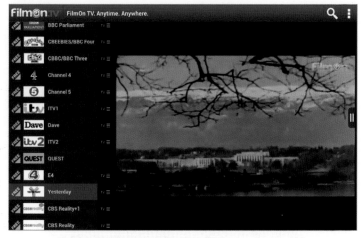

Fig. 6.9 The Yesterday Channel Screen on FilmOn TV.

As you can see, most of the **Freeview** channels are present and the TV Guide for the UK channels (obtained by tapping

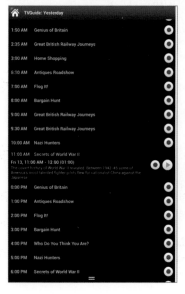

the [TV ≡] button, as shown in Fig. 6.9, is excellent, as is for Germany and Italy, but not so for other countries.

This is a worthwhile App to consider, particularly if you have interest in UK's **Freeview** channels, other countries' TV or live abroad and you don't want to pay a subscription fee for the privilege of watching the BBC channels!

Fig. 6.10 The TV Guide for the Yesterday Channel.

Installing a YouTube Video App

One of the easiest **YouTube** Apps to use for watching videos is the **InstaTube** shown here. It has the cleanest and most intuitive interface, but it is not free. The free version allows you to download up to 5 videos, after which you'll have to purchase the **Professional** version for £1.47 if you want to download more, but at least you can find out if you like the App before buying the full version. There is also a Kindle Fire version for £1.29.

To find it, go to the **Appstore** and search for **youtube app for kindle**. Amongst the many Apps that display on your screen, tap the icon of **InstaTube** to buy it and install it, then tap **Open** after installation is complete, to display a screen similar to that shown in Fig. 6.11.

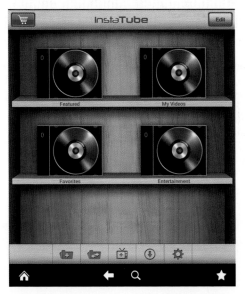

Fig. 6.11 Part of InstaTube App's Opening Screen.

The App has four default **Playlist** categories for keeping your collection of videos, namely **Featured**, **My Videos**, **Favorites** and **Entertainment**, but you can create more.

The five options at the bottom of the screen in Fig. 6.11 shown on the previous page, have the following functions:

Create a new Playlist.

Delete Playlists.

Select video source.

List all downloaded videos

Settings

It is worth trying all these options to get a feel of what they can do, but see below.

> **Note:** In **Settings** you are given the option to sign-in to the video sources. It is best, at this stage, not to sign-in as the App works perfectly well with all three video sources without doing so. In the case of **YouTube**, if you sign-in with a <u>non-gmail</u> e-mail address, the App will stop working correctly. Signing in allows you to access your own personal lists **Favorites**, **Watch** later, **Private Playlists**, **Subscriptions**, etc., on each of the video sources. If you don't have such personal lists it is best not to sign-in.
>
> .

To start with, use the **Select a video source** option which displays the screen in Fig. 6.12.

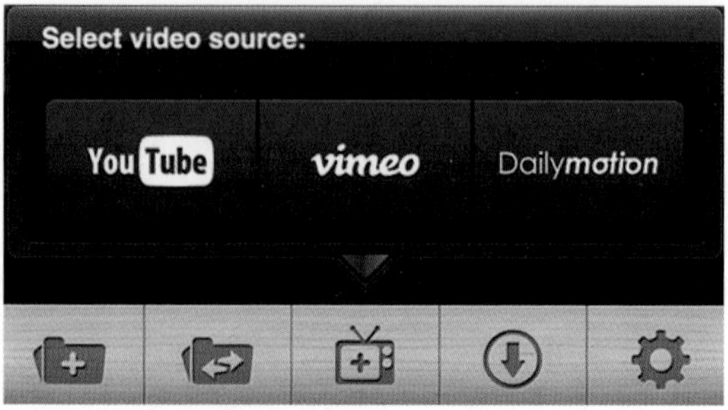

Fig. 6.12 Selecting a Video Source.

Choosing one of the three video sources, say **YouTube**, displays a **Categories** list for you to choose from, as shown in Fig. 6.13.

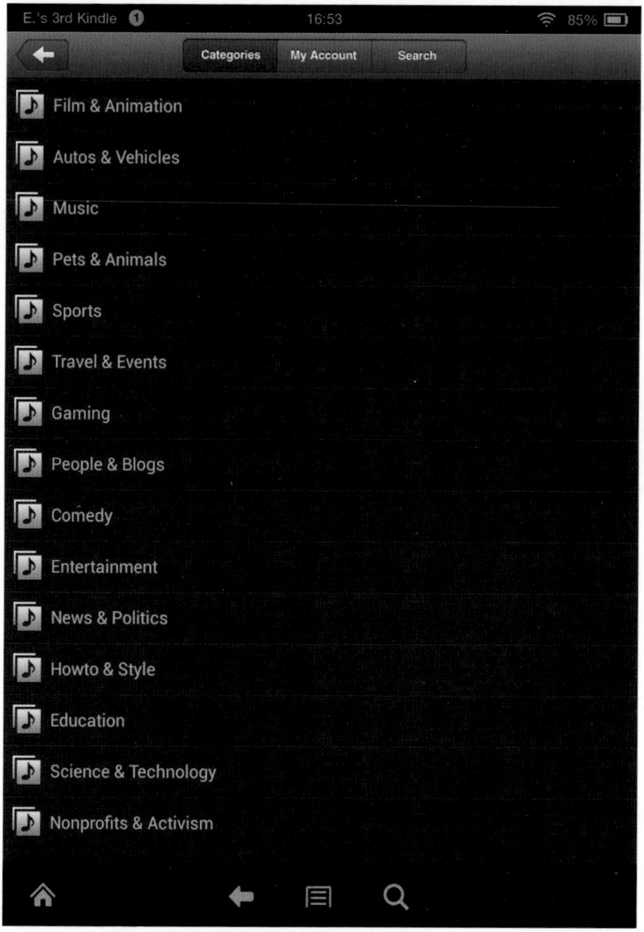

Fig. 6.13 Video Categories.

The Screen in Fig. 6.14 shown on the next page, displays a list of videos when the **Pets & Animals** category is selected in Fig. 6.13 above.

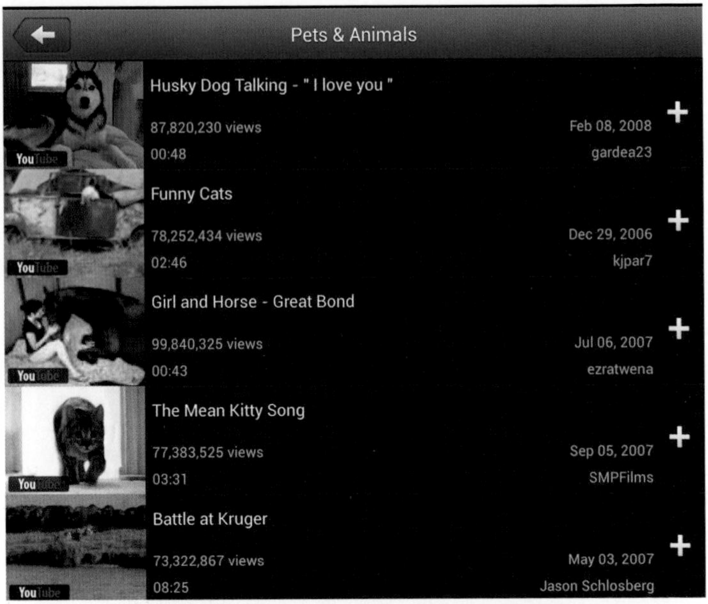

Fig. 6.14 A Smal Part of the Video List in Pets & Animals Category.

To select a video to add to one of your **Playlists**, tap the **Plus** ➕ button – you'll be asked to which **Playlist** you want to send the video, after which the sign against that video changes to a tick ✅. Now, tapping on the actual name of a marked video, downloads it and makes it ready for playing.

However, tapping the name of an unmarked video, it plays it without downloading it. You only download videos that you want to keep so that you can see them when away from a WiFi connection.

Tapping the **Go back** ⬅ button, at the top left of the screen, twice after playing a video, returns you to the **InstaTube** opening screen, except that now the playlist you chose to download the video into, includes the picture of one of your chosen videos.

This is a very interesting App, worth spending sometime getting to know it.

Games

Entertainment would not be complete without including games! The only problem here is the myriad of games available from which to make your personal choice.

To access games, go to **Home**, then tap on the **Games library** link as shown in Fig. 6.15 below. There is a vast choice of free games available, one of which is **Blendoku**.

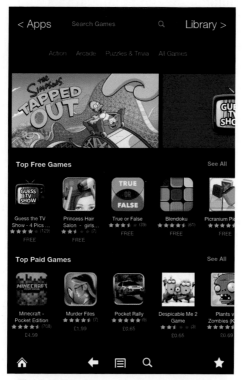

Fig. 6.15 The Games App Opening Screen.

This game appeals to me because it is a form of **Sudoku**, but instead of arranging numbers in some form of order, it requires you to arrange colours in a rainbow order instead.

The game is based on actual colour principles, challenging your ability to distinguish and arrange colours, a kind of **Sudoku**, crossword puzzle and colour flow, all in one mix.

The game has hundreds of levels of difficulty and is suitable for both children and adults. You are given a score for each success, in terms of time taken to complete each game, and with practice you are able to beat your own best score or the world average! The result of a medium level 1 success is shown below, which also beats the world average!

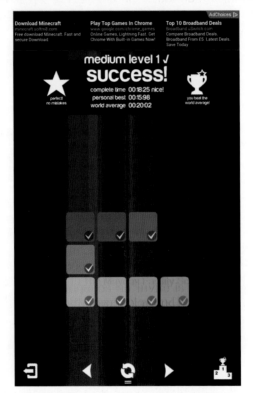

Fig. 6.16 The Game Blendoku in Operation.

There is a **Help** screen, as well as **Options** screen, but as it is very intuitive, I leave it to you to work your way through this addictive game!

Aeroplane Mode

All videos, games (and other items on the cloud) that were downloaded to your Kindle Fire, can be enjoyed when away from an Internet connection, for instance, when you are travelling and especially by air.

To prove that your collection of videos, games and other items will be available to you under such circumstances, go to the **Home** screen touch the time at the top of the screen and swipe downwards to display the **Device Control** screen shown in Fig. 6.17.

Fig. 6.17 The Device Control Screen.

Next, tap the **Wireless** option to reveal the screen, part of which is shown in Fig. 6.18 below.

Wireless

Aeroplane Mode   On   **Off**

Bluetooth   >

Wi-Fi   **On**   Off
Need help connecting to Wi-Fi?

Fig. 6.18 The Wireless Screen.

Now, tap the **Aeroplane Mode** to turn it to **On** which will automatically switch the **WiFi** connection to **Off**. Next, return to the **Home** screen, tap on the **Apps library** and start the **Videos** or **Games** Apps and see if you can play your videos or games.

After verification, don't forget to reverse the **Aeroplane Mode**, so that you can connect again to your **WiFi**. Enjoy your travelling time, but don't forget your headphones!

Note: You can use the **Aeroplane Mode** feature to switch off your WiFi connection when you don't need it. Being connected to the Internet tends to drain the Kindle's battery unnecessarily.

7

Tips On Reading Books

Don't worry, I am not going to tell you how to read books! What I am about to discuss here are some essentials which could make reading a book on the Kindle Fire HDX a better experience.

The Reading Toolbar

To see the **Reading Toolbar**, go to **Home**, then tap the **Books library** and find a free book (any will do) and open it. Next, tap the middle-top of a page, near where the time is normally shown on the screen, to display the **Reading Toolbar** as shown at the top of the screen in Fig. 7.1.

Fig. 7.1 The Reading Toolbar.

The Text Settings

To change text options such as **Font** size and type, **Margins**, etc., tap the **View** button which displays the screen shown in Fig. 7.2 below.

Fig. 7.2 The Text Settings.

The easiest way to change the **Font** size of a book is to tap the **Increase Font** button. Each time you tap this button the **Font** size increases by 1, so that size 7 Georgia shown above becomes 8. To decrease the font size tap the **Decrease Font** button. As you tap the **Increase** or **Decrease** button the action is reflected on the displayed page so you can see immediately whether you like the result.

You can also change the **Margins** from normal to wider spacing and **Line Spacing** from what it is to higher spacing. **Colour Mode** allows you to change the normal black letters on a white background to black letters on a sepia background or white letters on a black background.

Tapping the right-arrowhead ⟩ against the present **Font** (**Georgia**) in Fig. 7.2, gives you a list of four fonts to choose from, while tapping the **More Settings** link at the bottom of Fig. 7.2 above, displays the screen shown in Fig. 7.3 on the next page.

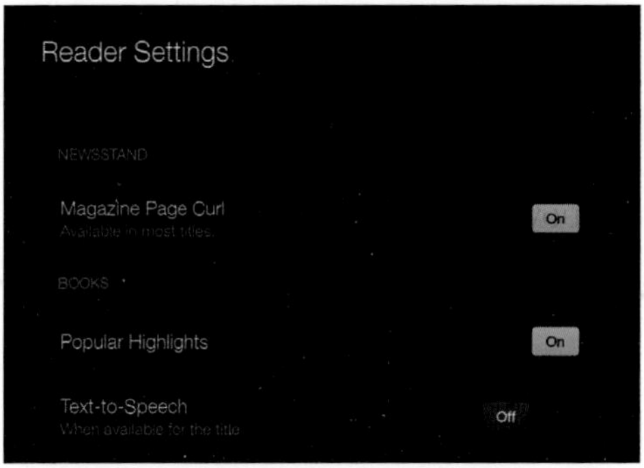

Fig. 7.3 The More Options Screen.

By default, **Popular Highlights** are **On** which allows you to highlight words that you choose. It places markers around the word you tap and hold and at the same time it displays an explanation of the meaning of the word you selected, as shown in Fig. 7.4. If now you select the **Full Definition** option at the bottom right of the screen, additional clarification on the meaning of the selected word can be obtain from **Dictionary Wikipedia** or **Translation** pages.

Fig. 7.4 Highlight and Definition of Chosen Word in Text.

If you want to highlight more words, drag the markers shown in Fig. 7.4 to cover all the required words, then tap one of the coloured squares, to highlight your selection with that colour.

To remove the highlighter, touch and hold anywhere within the highlighted selection, then tap the coloured button marked with X, as shown in Fig. 7.5.

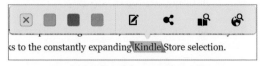

Fig. 7.5 Removing Highlighted Selection.

Next, tapping the **On** button against **Text-to-Speech** in Fig. 7.3 on the previous page, allows you to turn on a kind of audio player. All you need to do to listen to someone reading the text is to tap the black arrowhead at the bottom of the page shown in Fig. 7.6.

Fig. 7.6 Starting the Audio Player.

Navigation

As mentioned earlier, to see the **Reading Toolbar**, tap the middle-top of a page, near where the time is normally shown on the screen, to display it as shown in Fig. 7.7.

Fig. 7.7 The Reading Toolbar.

Next, tap the **Options** button at the extreme left of the screen above to display a screen similar to that of Fig. 7.8.

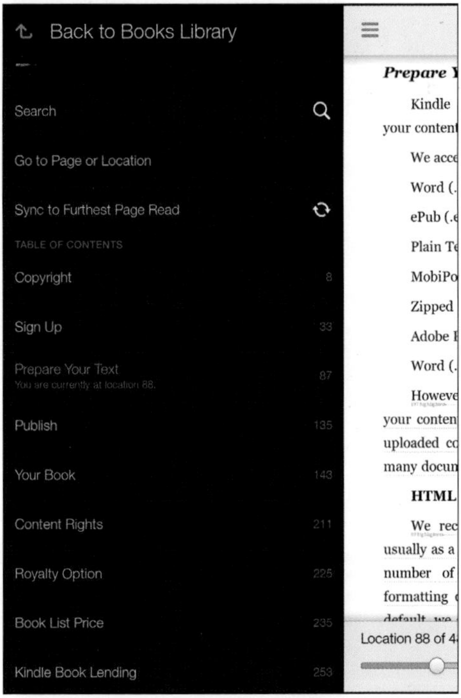

Fig. 7.8 The Go To Screen.

To go to any part of the book, just tap the appropriate entry. I find the **Contents** page (if the book has one) a good place to choose as there are links there to tap that will take you exactly where you want to go.

Notes and Marks

Notes can be created at any point in a book so that you can refer to them later. To add a note, touch and hold on a word at the beginning of a sentence, then drag the marker to cover your selection and tap the **Pencil** icon shown in Fig. 7.9 which opens a **Notes** window for you to type your comment and **Save** it.

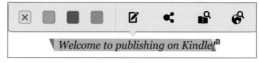

Fig. 7.9 Marking a Sentence to Create a Note.

As an example I made one note shown as the first entry in Fig. 7.10, while the rest of the notes are those made by the author of the book. Tap **Notes** on the **Reading Toolbar**.

My Notes & Marks	X
Welcome to publishing on Kindle!	
Highlight	Location 15
Good news!	
Note	Location 15
However, for best results, we suggest that you upload your content in HTML format, as Amazon KDP converts all uploaded content into HTML first. You can export or save many documents as HTML from inside Microsoft Word. HTML	
Popular Highlight - 197 highlighters	Location 98
We recommend uploading content in HTML format, usually as a single .html file. Please note that KDP supports a number of select HTML tags, but that most complex formatting options do not translate well to the reader. By default, we suggest that you u...	
Popular Highlight - 80 highlighters	Location 102
If your HTML content contains images or multiple files you'll need to compress all files into a .zip file before uploading. All the files in the .zip archive must be in a single folder, without any files (like images) in sub-folders. If your content ...	
Popular Highlight - 84 highlighters	Location 114

Fig. 7.10 The Notes Produced by the Author of a Book.

Notes created by the author of a book cannot be edited or deleted. You can only edit or delete notes you have created yourself by touching and holding on the blue image against your note, then selecting **Edit** or **Delete** from the displayed menu.

The X-Ray Feature

The **X-Ray** feature used to be confined exclusively to books, but lately has been extended to films as well. However, not all books or films support **X-Ray** concepts as I found out when I tried it on the book I have been using as an example.

There is, however, another book in my Kindle Fire library that supports **X-Ray** concepts, so I'll use that book to explain how it works. Below, I display a passage from that book with the two names mentioned in it highlighted purely for your convenience.

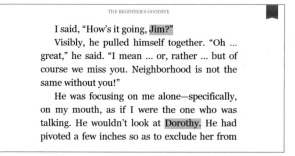

Fig. 7.11 A Book Passage That Supports X-Ray Concepts.

While reading a book like the one above, tap the middle of the page, then tap **X-Ray** on the displayed **Reading Toolbar**. What appears then on the screen is shown in Fig. 7.12 for the **Current Page** of this book.

Fig. 7.12 Some of the X-Ray Results of Specified Persons.

What I show here are the names of Jim and Dorothy with a type of frequency bar which shows all the locations in the book where that name (it could also be a term) is mentioned in the book. Tapping on this bar, say for Jim, displays the following screen.

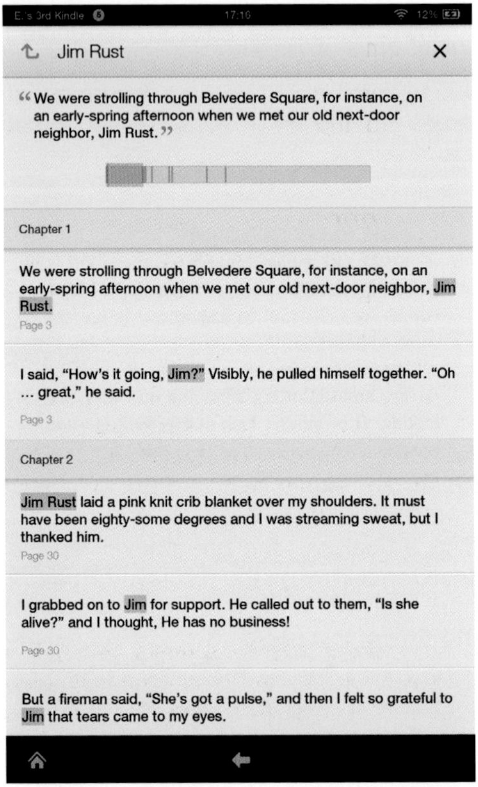

Fig. 7.13 The Pages where Jim is mentioned in the Book.

You'll have to scroll down to see all the references in the entire book relating to this person.

You could list all the names of **All** the people plus **Terms** in the book by tapping **All** (32 in this book) or just **People** (26 in this book) or **Terms** (6 in this book) as shown at the very top in Fig. 7.12 on the previous page.

In the case of films, you can find out an actor's name, his biography, in which other roles or scenes he has acted without having to halt the film. Again, not all films are **X-Ray** capable.

In addition to books and films, the **X-Ray** feature also appears in some textbooks. If available, you can follow links to view more information on Wikipedia or on YouTube.

To return to where you were in the book before stating the **X-Ray** feature, tap the **Back** arrow as many times as necessary.

The Sharing Option

The Sharing option on the **Reading Toolbar** allows you to share highlights and notes on **Facebook** and **Twitter**.

I suppose expressing one's opinion in social media might help others to make an informed opinion of a book. I find, however, that very few such comments are of any real value. More useful comments can be found in 'archives of book reviews' written by experienced critics. Try searching the Internet – you'll find lots of sites that specialise on this subject.

Bookmarks

Bookmarks are used to mark the place you got to when reading a book. To insert a bookmark, tap the middle-top of the page to display the **Reading Toolbar**, then tap the **Bookmark** option shown here.

Next time you go back to the same book, it will open at the last inserted **Bookmark**, as shown in Fig. 7.14 below, so you never lose your place.

THE BEGINNER'S GOODBYE

I said, "How's it going, Jim?"
Visibly, he pulled himself together. "Oh ... great," he said. "I mean ... or, rather ... but of course we miss you. Neighborhood is not the same without you!"

Fig. 7.14 Book Marking a Sentence.

Additional Reading Features

While you are reading a book, you have additional features available to you to make the experience more enjoyable.

Page Numbers and Page Locations

Not all Kindle Fire books include page numbers, but if they do, it will be mentioned on the **Product Details** page with the words 'Page Numbers Source' preceding the ISBN number of the book. Page numbers are normally placed at the same position as in printed books.

Page location on the other hand marks the location of each line of text and can be displayed by tapping the centre of the screen (while reading), to display the location numbers at the bottom-left of the screen, as shown in Fig. 7.15.

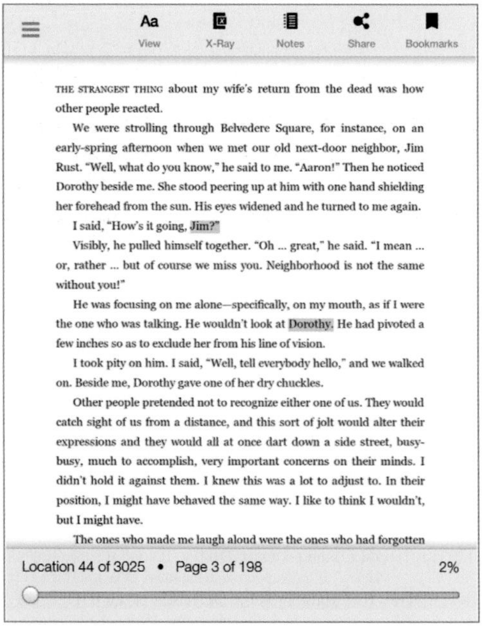

Fig. 7.15 Location Numbers at Bottom-left.

The location in the book shown on the screen of Fig. 7.15, can be found just above the player and reads as **Location 44 of 3025**, **Page 3 of 198**. Also note that at the bottom-right of the page of the book, the percentage of the book read so far is displayed, in this case **2%**.

Zooming In on Images

If there is an image on the page you are reading you can tap on the image to increase its size (zoom in). To return to the normal image size (zoom out), tap it again.

You can also use the finger movements described on page 12 to zoom in or out.

Reading in the Dark

If you are one of these people who find comfort in reading when you can't sleep in the middle of the night and don't want to disturb your sleeping partner, then perhaps you might like to know how to dim the screen of your Kindle Fire.

The background light of the Kindle Fire in the middle of the night is like a beacon. To tone it down, touch and hold on the time at the top of the screen, then swipe downwards to display the **Device Control** screen, tap the **Brightness** option to display what is shown in Fig. 7.16.

Fig. 7.16 The Device Control Screen.

Next, tap the **Off** button against the **Auto-Brightness**, if **On**.

This should reduce the brightness of the backlit screen quite a bit, but still not enough. To make it more comfortable for both your sleeping partner and yourself, slide the slider to the left to reduce brightness to almost zero.

I find that reducing brightness to almost zero, makes it difficult to read. To overcome this, tap the middle-top of a page, near where the time is normally shown on the screen, to display the **Reading Toolbar** as shown in Fig. 7.17.

Fig. 7.17 The Reading Toolbar.

Next, tap the **View** option to display the screen in Fig. 7.18.

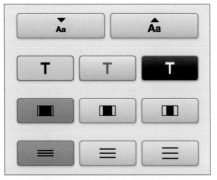

Fig. 7.18 The Text Settings.

Finally, change the **Colour Mode** by tapping on the **Black** button with the white letter **T**. This changes the book's background to black with white letters. The page now is acceptable for night-time reading, as the glaring white backlit screen has been replaced by a black background and the only light comes from the actual letters which makes them easier to read under normal brightness.

Do remember to do all this before going to bed, however, and not in the middle of the night! Enjoy your reading.

8

OfficeSuite Professional 7

The Kindle Fire comes equipped with **OfficeSuite** by **Mobile Systems,** which allows you to read Microsoft Office documents. To find it, go to **Home**, then **Apps** and tap the **Device tab**. Amongst the Apps already on your device you'll find **OfficeSuite's**, starting image button, as shown here.

If, on the other hand, you want to be able to edit or create Microsoft Office documents you'll need to buy **OfficeSuite Pro 7**. To find it, go to **Home**, then **Apps** and tap the **Store** link. Next, search the **Appstore** for **OfficeSuite Pro** which finds the App amongst others, as shown on a partial screen similar to that in Fig. 8.1 below.

Fig. 8.1 Some Apps found by Search for OfficeSuite Pro.

> **Note:** Although **OfficeSuite Professional 7** appears more expensive than adjacent Apps, it does include a suite of programs, namely **Word**, **Excel**, **PowerPoint** and an excellent **User's guide**.

Tap on the icon of **OfficeSuite Professional 7** to buy it and install it, then tap **Open**, after installation, to display a screen similar to that shown in Fig. 8.2.

Fig. 8.2 The OfficeSuite Pro 7 Opening Screen.

While you are in a spending mood, you might consider two more optional Apps that will supplement **OfficeSuite Pro**. These are shown in Fig. 8.3 below.

Fig. 8.3 Optional Apps.

The **OfficeSuite Font Package** integrates with **Office Pro 7** and can only be opened within it. The package gives genuine compatibility with **Word** documents. It includes **Arial**, **Calibri**, **Courier New**, and **Times New Roman**, all with regular fonts, bold, italic and bold italic typefaces, plus a set of four **Wingdings** symbol characters. The package is compatible with **OfficeSuite Pro** version 6.10 or higher. The reason for its low rating is that people tried to use it with earlier versions of **OfficeSuite Pro** or decided that the font package should have been included in the price of **OfficeSuite Pro 7**. Read the reviews to see this for yourself.

The **QuickSpell** App is self-explanatory!

Package Overview

When opened, **OfficeSuite Pro 7** displays the screen in Fig. 8.2 shown on the previous page. The **Home** menu option on the left of the screen displays what you see on the right of the screen, which is the three modules that comprise the **OfficeSuite Pro** plus the **User's guide** (swipe to the left to see more pages).

This and the other options available on the left of the opening screen, shown below, have the functions stated and when activated display appropriate folders or files on the right of the screen.

Create new documents in Word, Excel or PowerPoint by selecting the appropriate module.

Browse recently used document files.

Create new documents from supplied templates.

The default document folder containing your files.

Folders and files saved in internal memory storage.

Folders and files saved on a remote server such as **SkyDrive** in the 'Cloud'.

The above facilities will be discussed when and where the subject comes up while examining the individual modules that make up the **OfficeSuite Pro 7**. In the mean time, you might like to tap each option in turn to see what displays on the right of the screen when each is activated.

The Office Menu Options

At the top right of the screen in Fig. 8.2 shown on page 106, you can see three stacked white squares. When tapped, a menu of options applicable to the whole **OfficeSuite** package is displayed as shown in Fig. 8.4 below.

Tapping the **Settings** menu option, displays the screen shown in Fig. 8.5.

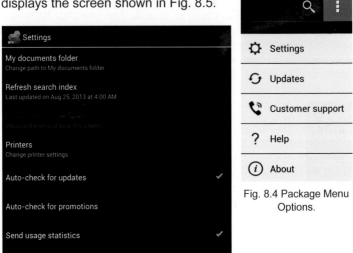

Fig. 8.4 Package Menu Options.

Fig. 8.5 The Settings Menu Options.

It might be a good idea to tap the square against the **Auto-check for updates** options to place a check mark, as shown above. You'll also see that the option to **Download font package** is greyed out because I have already done so.

To check where your documents are saved, tap the **My documents folder** which displays the screen shown in Fig. 8.6.

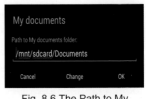

Don't bother about the **Printers** option, unless you intend to save your documents to **Google Docs** and print them from there. I shall only use my **HP e-Printer**.

Fig. 8.6 The Path to My Documents Folder.

The OfficeSuite's Word Module

Word is part of the **OfficeSuite Pro 7** package and is compatible with **Microsoft's Word**. It is capable of reading. editing and creating the latest **Word** (**.docx**), **Word 97-2003** (**.doc**), **Rich Text Format** (**.rtf**) and **Plain text** (**.txt**) documents.

Word, just as **Microsoft's Word**, has strong leanings towards desk top publishing which offers fully editable WYSIWYG (what you see is what you get) modes. Couple this with the ability to include and manipulate full colour graphics and to easily create **Shapes**, **Tables**, **Hyperlinks**, **Comments**, **Footnotes** and **Endnotes** and you can see the enormous power of the program.

You will find using **Word** to be intuitive and easy and you will soon be producing the type of word processed output you would not have dreamed possible. Of course, if you are used to using **Microsoft's Word**, you will find that most of what is presented here rather familiar, except for the fact that this version of **Word** is especially designed for the tablet.

Starting the Word Module

Word is started by either tapping on its icon when you first start **OfficeSuite Pro 7** (see Fig. 8.2, page 106) or tapping **My documents** and selecting a **Word** file from the displayed list, as shown in Fig. 8.7, provided you have already saved one there.

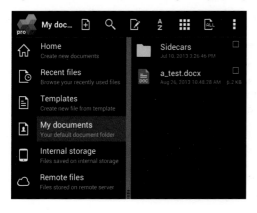

Fig. 8.7 Selecting a Saved Document from My Documents Folder.

The Word Screen

The opening **Word** screen, after typing a few words, is shown in Fig. 8.8. Perhaps you could spend some time familiarising yourself with the various parts of this screen.

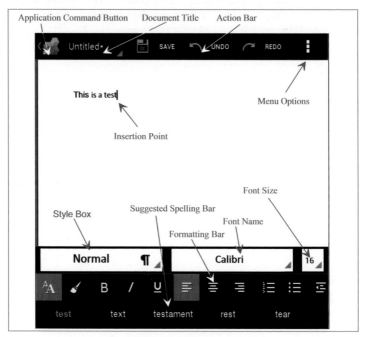

Fig. 8.8 The Word Screen Layout.

Obviously, before you type a few words in **Word**, the opening 'blank' screen will not display the **Style** box, **Font** name and size or the suggested **Spelling** bar.

Do investigate the **Action** bar's **Menu** options to see for yourself what their sub-menus can offer. Also, you might like to have a look at the formatting bar which allows you to create professional looking documents.

Finally before printing your documents, do check your spelling! I leave it to you to experiment with creating and formatting **Word** documents.

The OfficeSuite's Excel Module

The **Excel** module in **OfficeSuite** is a powerful electronic spreadsheet capable of creating and solving budgeting, scientific and engineering problems. It is fully compatible with **Microsoft's Excel** and capable of reading, editing and creating the latest **Excel Workbook** (**.xlsx**), **Excel 97-2003** (**.xls**), and **CSV comma delimited** (**.csv**) files. Its opening screen is shown in Fig. 8.9 below.

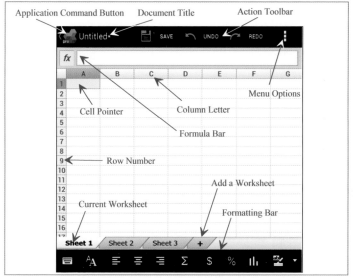

Fig. 8.9 The Excel Screen Layout.

Note: The on-screen keyboard only displays when you double-tap in a cell to enter information.

Excel Overview

When you first enter **Excel**, the program sets up a series of huge electronic pages, or worksheets, in your Kindle's memory, many times larger than the small part shown on the screen. Individual cells are identified by column and row location (in that order).

A worksheet can be thought of as a two-dimensional table made up of rows and columns. The point where a row and column intersect is called a cell, while the reference points of a cell are known as the cell address. The active cell (A1 when you first enter the program) is boxed.

To move around a worksheet, scroll with your finger or with a stylus. The area within which you can move the active cell is referred to as the working area of the worksheet, while the letters and numbers in the border at the top and left of the working area give the 'co-ordinates' of the cells in a worksheet.

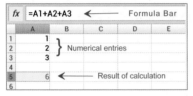

Fig. 8.10 The Formula Bar.

The contents of a cell are displayed above the column letters within the **Formula Bar**. If you type text in the active cell, it appears in both the **Formula Bar** and the cell itself.

Typing a formula which is preceded by the equals sign (=) to, say, add the contents of three cells, causes the actual formula to appear in the **Formula Bar**, while the result of the actual calculation appears in the active cell when the Next key on the on-screen keyboard is tapped.

A workbook can have more than one worksheet, as shown in Fig. 8.9 on the previous page. On that screen, three worksheet tabs are shown with names 'Sheet 1', 'Sheet 2' and 'Sheet 3', with the current active worksheet being 'Sheet 1'. To move to another worksheet from the current worksheet, just tap its tab. To create a new worksheet, tap the ⟨ + ⟩ tab.

Obviously there is a lot more to worksheets, including the ability to use functions to carry out extremely complex calculations, forecasts and numerous other types of modelling. You can also create charts to view numerical results in graphical form. It is worth, if you are interested, pursuing these studies, but as far as this book is concerned, I have reached the end of the allocated space.

OfficeSuite's PowerPoint Module

The **PowerPoint** module in **OfficeSuite** is a powerful graphics **Presentation** package which allows you to create a slide show and the production of ancillary material, such as scripted notes to accompany each slide, laser copies of slides, and an outline view of all the information in the presentation.

The module is fully compatible with **Microsoft's PowerPoint** and capable of reading, editing and creating the latest **PowerPoint Presentation (.pptx)**, the **PowerPoint Presentation 97-2003 (.ppt)** and the equivalent **PowerPoint Show** files. Its opening screen is shown in Fig. 8.11 below.

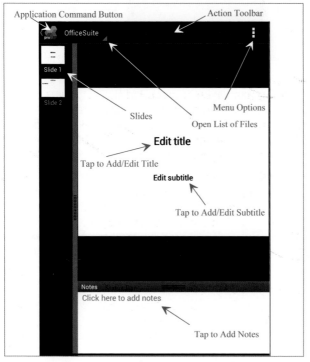

Fig. 8.11 The PowerPoint Screen Layout.

Note: The on-screen keyboard only displays when you double-tap to add or edit a title or subtitle (Fig. 8.11) and you then tap the pencil button on the displayed pop-up shown here. The other option in the pop-up displays the **Shape properties** box shown in Fig. 8.12.

Shape properties

Line

O

Line style: Solid

Line width: ——

Fill

●

Cancel   OK

Fig. 8.12 The Shape Properties Box.

Selecting the **Line** option allows you to choose what type of line to use, whether solid, dot, dash dot, etc., while selecting the **Fill** option displays an array of colours to choose from.

You could also add photos to your creation by tapping the second slide in the opening screen (see Fig. 8.11 on the previous page) and use the **Menu**, **Insert**, **Picture** option.

Once you are satisfied with what you have achieved so far, tap the **Save** button which displays the **Save as** box ready for you to give your work a name.

> **Note:** In general, **OfficeSuite Pro 7** is an extremely useful program, particularly if you want to edit **Word**, **Excel** or **PowerPoint** documents that you created on a computer. However, creating complicated documents on the Kindle Fire using **OfficeSuite Pro** has its limitations, as no doubt you'll find out, if you ventured in that direction. This is to be expected running a program on such a limited size screen using a finger or stylus that is much wider than the delicate work you are trying to do. Having said that, I find the program invaluable and worth giving it a try. Good luck!

Index